MW00806705

What a deep and powerful journey Catherine Anderson takes us on in her beautifully written book, *My Brother Speaks in Dreams*. I was instantly engaged as her story unfolded, showing us the difficulties of loving, accepting, learning from, and living with a beautiful soul who thinks and communicates differently. Anderson's authentic voice, her intricate introspections, and her empathetic observations make this unique tale a universal story. The characters, issues, stigmas, confusions, and deep connections stayed with me long after I turned the final page.
—Deborah Shouse, author of *Love in the Land of Dementia: Finding Hope in the Caregiver's Journey*.

꜍❀꜠꜠❀꜠

Catherine Anderson's memoir about life with her neurodivergent brother, Charlie, is both gripping and poignant. It is well written, intimately considered, and revealing, an unflinching portrait of a unique family and brother facing uncommon circumstances over changing eras and environments. As the parent of an adult special needs child of my own, I appreciate well how daunting and challenging such a lifelong journey can be. Anderson navigates hers with Charlie with the sensitivity and understanding that only a sibling can share. Without exception, she does so with honesty, insight, respect, and perhaps most importantly, deep compassion and love.
——William Cass, author of *Something Like Hope & Other Stories*

Anderson speaks with eloquence about "the complexities of loving a child with intellectual disabilities in a world that rejects such imperfection." Ultimately, sometimes through tears, the reader will come to know intimately what life with Charlie taught the author and what her insights can teach us: that language is only one way to communicate, and our culture often fails to recognize and honor other ways.
—Maril Crabtree, author of *Fireflies in the Gathering Dark*

꙳ ❦ ♡ ❦ ꙳

Catherine Anderson writes she has "arms permanently open to catch whatever falls" in her intimate telling of the universal story of growing up with a sibling who is neurodivergent. The reader feels her mother's desperation to teach her son fluent speech, and the family's trauma of separation and shame when her sibling is sent away to "school." Our country's recent history of institutionalizing children like Charlie was driven by ignorance. Born in this century, the resources available to Charlie and his family would have altered the paths of all their lives and their ability to connect with each other. Catherine's deep love for her brother ultimately motivates her to learn his language in order to connect. She is shaped not only by her responsibilities but the common humanity of their relationship. *My Brother Speaks in Dreams* is a beautifully written memoir that will feel personal to some and profound to all.
—Jeanne Henry Hoose, retired special educator

MY BROTHER SPEAKS IN DREAMS

MY BROTHER SPEAKS IN DREAMS

Of Family, Beauty and Belonging

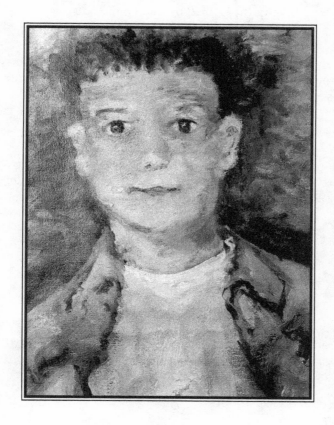

Catherine Anderson

Wising Up Press

Wising Up Press
P.O. Box 2122
Decatur, GA 30031-2122
www.universaltable.org

Copyright © 2022 by Catherine Anderson

All rights reserved. No part of this book may be used or reproduced in any manner whatsoever without written permission, except in the case of brief quotations embodied in critical articles or reviews.

ISBN: 978-1-7376940-3-8

Catalogue-in-Publication data is on file with the Library of Congress.
LCCN: 2022942262

In memory of Donna Lunn

Contents

We are tied together in the single garment of destiny, caught in an inescapable network of mutuality. And whatever affects one directly affects all indirectly.
Dr. Martin Luther King Jr.

As I Knew Him

My brother Charlie died in 2016. When we lose someone, we try to catch reams of events and conversations before they vanish because we don't want our loved one to become a person no one remembers. To remember a man like Charlie who was on the autistic spectrum with cognitive and speech barriers, the rush is intense. He didn't read or write. He never married, he never had children. Our intimacies were private and subtle. He spoke by repeating words spoken to him—quick, emphatic echoes, vivid and succinct, a kind of poetry. I knew my brother the full fifty-nine years of his life, one that touched me so deeply I've never experienced a day I haven't thought about him and the gifts he brought to the world.

Charlie and I were two and a half years apart in age, born in the 1950s. When my brother was eight years old, he had to leave us for an institution for children with intellectual disabilities where he lived until he was sixteen. When it closed down my parents arranged for him to live with us in Kansas City, and then in group homes throughout his adulthood. He was a member of a particular cohort in a particular point in time—the first group of former residents of an institution, a state home, to be welcomed back into a community that had once shunned him and those like him. I was fortunate to witness the blooming of a person who in another time would have withered behind institution walls.

My brother came into this world on a mythic bolt, and then left us just as dramatically. He was a week away from an appointment with a gastroenterologist when he died in his bed of undiagnosed gastric ulcers. No one knew how sick he was because in our attempt to help him, we missed nonverbal cues that could have revealed his symptoms. As his sister, and the one who knew him the longest, I deeply regret not understanding those signs.

When the spirit moved him, Charlie communicated his passions not only through the echoes of words but through his wide, embracing smile. He also spoke the spare, resonant language of pictures. That Charlie was able during his lifetime to find a place in this challenging world was remarkable. Anyone who knows someone with a communication difference has witnessed how difficult it is for that person to become visible, to be known and understood. Among his many lessons, I've received from Charlie an understanding that language moves beyond a simple transference of words and includes tone, gesture and expression. Nonverbal language speaks an entire universe of culture, if we pay attention. From knowing my brother, I've learned the importance of advocacy for language access, whether it be for interpreters and translators for non-English speakers or for better medical practices when serving someone with a communication disability. Each person has a right to be understood. It's a matter of justice, one that requires constant vigilance by all of us.

My brother was born into a family who took years to understand him. How we did is the heart of this story. Our understanding of joy, beauty, sadness and loss evolved the longer we knew him. The story told here is as much and even more about how my brother shaped the person I came to be, as it is about him. The only language I've ever found to tell it originates from powers of lyric, narrative, and image. The approach I've taken is to explore our relationship in the threshold between language and experience, the light and the dark, where a sense of a common beauty dwells. I'm a neurotypical observer, however, and my words are limited to what I felt and saw of our lives together. In these pages, my portrait of Charlie remains an approximation. I hope it's one he and many others who enriched his life would recognize.

I
HOUSE ON FERRIS STREET

♪♪ ✤ ❧ ✤ ❧ ✤ ♪♪

THE BREAD OF CHILDHOOD

Born among wolves, we learned grace.
Born in a time of fire, we slipped
through ice, tiny things
the weight of sand.

Names rained down like the sweat of Zeus.
We ignored them all and swallowed
the spark-flicker, shook foil
of things—salt diamonds dancing

on a crystal floor.
In childhood, the sun
cast a Leica sheen on all minutiae—
the wondrous Mrs. Z inhaling

a Lark behind the grocery counter
on old Moravian Drive,
her scarlet babushka and ring of blonde.
We entered her store and smelled

the bright scent of bread
wrapped in circus colors, laid out
like babies in a delivery ward.
Turning down the aisle with our eyes closed,

we thought this bread was infinite.

Myths and Origins

The cold night of my brother's birth resonated like a myth in our family. We told the story over and over. We could never stop telling it because we knew no other way of understanding what had happened. Our account of Charlie's birth carried all the textures of old mythology: the time before, paradisal, and the time after, sadness and bewilderment. Like a myth, the narrative was at once blurred and detailed with no clear evil identified to help predict a pattern sparing us a future round of damage. The theme emerging in each retelling was awe before a power no one understood and no one could control. In the following months and years after Charlie's birth when it was clear he was not developing normally, that feeling of helplessness was constant. My parents would say his birth transformed our whole family; we were completely different from any other generation before us.

This was decades before we were able to see Charlie's uniqueness as a strength, a human quality, and accept him for who he was, just as he was.

In the beginning, the details were ordinary. On the front of my brother's birth certificate is a handsome rendering of Harper Hospital in Detroit, Michigan, a seven-story brick building with an American flag flying in front. Below, in black Gothic script is the testament of the birth of Charles Edward Anderson on Sunday, the 27th day of January, 1957. The time of birth is 7:28 a.m. The birth certificate is signed by "the Director who has caused the Corporate Seal of this Hospital to be hereunto affixed." What has always intrigued me is the flip side, with my mother and father's names, my brother's weight of 7 pounds, 15 ounces, my mother's fingerprints at the bottom, and symmetrically balanced to the left and right, my brother's infant palm prints, resembling two gray stones. Over sixty years old, the birth certificate, printed on thick vellum, is only slightly yellowed, and the Hospital's affixed golden seal remains as shiny as the day my brother was born. The signature of the doctor, often blamed by my parents for neglect during what was a difficult birth, is written at the bottom in green ink: Owen C. Foster, M.D.

Another image, a memory I have right before my brother was born: I was over two years old, standing up in the front seat of the blue '52 Studebaker while my father drove. Car seats for children had not been invented yet. I faced backwards to watch the cars flowing behind us, shouting when a car was right up on us in an effort to help my father drive. My world was about to change. I was the first child in the family, drawing rapt attention from my mother, my father, and my grandparents who lived north of us, in Saginaw. What else I saw was a bassinet lying on the back seat of the car. "It's a bed for the new baby," my father told me when I asked. I recall staring and staring at the woven bassinet, imagining a baby asleep in this bed, smaller than mine.

My blurred recollection of the night of Charlie's birth included a young child's version of adventure: staying with two boys a little older than me, wearing a plaid bathrobe and playing with trucks. My parents' version of the story was, of course, much more complex. I once asked my father, then almost eighty years old, and long after my mother had died, to tell me again what he thought happened the night of Charlie's birth that could have caused his disability. My father recounted the ice and wind on the road that night and the difficult time he had driving from our house on Ferris Street into Detroit where Harper Hospital was located, about eighteen miles away. I had heard the story years ago, but it sounded almost new in this recollection. "The car door handle on your mother's side was frozen and your mother had to hold it shut all the way to the hospital. It was a miserable drive." He blamed himself for not being able to thaw the door handle and believed the stress on my mother may have complicated the birth. Archived weather reports from January 26 through 27 in 1957 validate my father's memory. The weather had been blustery, snowy, with temperatures low enough to freeze a car door handle.

The doctor was late to arrive at the hospital, according to my mother. He never examined her before she went into delivery. In the manner of most women in 1957 who gave birth in a hospital, my mother was totally unconscious at the time Charlie was born. I believe she must have been given twilight sleep, a combination of morphine and scopolamine commonly used in the 1950s to ease childbirth pain. During some of the restless hours she was in labor, my mother told me, the nurses allowed her to get up, walk around, and climb back in a bed, she remembered, with sides to it. I learned later that those sides were for preventing a woman from falling out in reaction to the powerful hallucinations twilight sleep sometimes induced. When her labor increased, the sedative mix was most likely administered. My mother said she didn't remember a thing other than waking to hear she had given birth to a new baby boy. Eventually my parents would learn their baby had been born oxygen-deprived, what was then called a "blue baby." Following the practice of hospitals in the 1950s, my brother was held in a heated incubator for those first few hours after birth while my mother slept. My father, of course, was not allowed in the hospital room where the childbirth took place.

At the time, no one asked questions about a baby born blue. This was a mistake. My parents had always believed oxygen deprivation was the cause of Charlie's disability, described by doctors as "mental retardation and mental illness." My father told me he was once assigned to write an article on Harper Hospital for *The Detroit News*, where he worked as a reporter. This was when Charlie was about seven years old and not developing normally. In the interview, a spokesman extolled the hospital's progress in medical treatment. "I wanted to punch him out," my usually calm father told me. But he and my mother never brought their concerns to the hospital, both believing to complain about an unidentified birth defect would lead nowhere. Whether or not my brother's birth as a blue baby caused his future disabilities would never be resolved. My parents kept the myth of Charlie's damaging birth alive for years as they struggled for an explanation of his disability. Myth brings the "unknown into relation with the known," as one classics scholar has phrased it. My parents were like people from an ancient time who searched and searched the sky to understand events that couldn't be explained.

In the beginning, before he was two years old, and the signs of something askew in his development emerged, my brother Charlie was a wonder, a baby with large brown eyes and a head full of blond curls so endearing people would stop on the street, and tell my mother, "Don't ever cut his hair!" Our great-aunt Doll on my father's side recalled a letter my father wrote in which he boasted, "Now I have a little boy!" My grandfather, too, was so thrilled he set aside a bag of silver dollars for Charlie's future, passed down from grandfather to grandson. I was also enchanted from the moment I saw my baby brother in my mother's arms. My mother enjoyed telling me how I'd remind her not to drop him, to wrap him in a blanket, to make sure to feed him. A picture of him as a toddler shows a chubby little boy wearing overalls with a pair of boxer gloves on the front. My father is standing next to him; it's a black and white photo taken by one of the newspaper photographers. I don't remember telling my mother how to take care of a baby, but I do recall that pair of corduroy pants.

What I didn't know as a young child and learned later from my mother was the time Charlie, only a few weeks old and not yet baptized, seemed to have stopped breathing, turning blue again. "I sprinkled water from the kitchen sink on him, saying the words of a provisional baptism because I thought he might die." My mother was never overtly religious, so this act must have been one of extreme urgency. She told me he seemed to exhibit no immediate effect. And then she had nothing more to say about the event. I don't know if she rushed him to the pediatrician's office (she didn't have a car) or if she mentioned it later to the doctor. Throughout Charlie's babyhood and childhood, she had to be alert to any change in his physical behavior that would indicate an illness he couldn't describe due to his limited speech and cognitive ability. As he grew older, she seemed to be aware of a fragility in him only she could detect. I would learn later, after she died and Charlie was under my guardianship, that her intuitions were very accurate.

When my parents married in 1952, my mother, Doris Mae Johnson, a native of Tampa, moved north to Detroit with my father who had already started to work for *The Detroit News*. Her first shock was snow, falling in light flakes or accumulating on top of a train car. She discovered pine trees, ice skates, and how to keep milk fresh on a window sill if you didn't own an electric refrigerator. This was quite a change from her life growing up in semi-tropical Florida with her sister and two brothers. When they married, my mother, raised as a Protestant, took classes to convert to my father's Catholic religion. A graduate of Florida State University, my mother was a school speech therapist, or speech correctionist, as her profession was called then. She was eager to carry on her work in Detroit.

My father, James Keith Anderson, an only child born in Grand Junction, Colorado, moved twenty-three times in his childhood during the Great Depression because his father struggled to find work as a chemist. They often lived in boarding houses throughout the Midwest where my father sometimes slept on two kitchen chairs pushed together to make a bed. They finally settled in Saginaw where my father graduated from high school. He served in the infantry in World War II, fighting in five battles of the European theater. Under the G.I. Bill, he went to the University of Michigan and studied history and then became a newspaper reporter. My father came to Tampa to report on organized crime uncovered by the Kefauver hearings of the early 1950s and met my mother through her two brothers, both attorneys. Later he would cover the diverse ethnic communities of Detroit, focusing on new immigrants from Eastern Europe, the Middle East, and Latin America, as well as the Black community.

Like Charlie, I was born in Harper Hospital, not far from my parents' apartment on Holcomb Street where I lived my first year. In 1955, my father, again with assistance from the G. I. Bill, bought the first single-family house he had ever lived in, a three-bedroom ranch on Ferris Street in Mt. Clemens, Michigan. The irony—my father's ability to find a home at an affordable rate while the communities he reported on in central Detroit were excluded due to red-lining—was one my parents, of their time, probably didn't realize. This racial inequity would come to light years later in the Detroit uprising of 1967.

I hold another memory in my mind that refuses to fade, one that occurred on a beautiful Sunday afternoon when it became clear something was definitely wrong with Charlie. We were at a picnic held by the local Middle Eastern community on the shores of Lake St. Clair. At the picnic, immigrant leaders would be giving speeches my father covered for his column, "Cosmopolitan Detroit." I must have been six years old and Charlie about three. Our little brother Billy had not yet been born. At the time, Charlie was given to temper tantrums that could go on without stopping until my mother put him to bed. Throughout the lively afternoon, my mother had been pointing out a new baby to him in an attempt to help him connect with the surrounding world. She had been encouraged by his recent curiosity about other children. I stood next to my father, enchanted by the sound of men speaking in accented English while my father rapidly took notes until I broke away to run through the grass. A little later I walked into the tent where everyone gathered out of the sun. I heard my parents' voices, now very solemn. I grabbed a piece of honey-coated baklava and saw my mother, her eyes red. Was she crying? I wondered. I'd never seen her like this before. Outside the tent I could hear the noise of people laughing and clapping to the music of an accordion, such a contrast to the somber talk inside. "We have to leave, Cathy," my mother said. "Charlie slapped the little baby in the face." My mother must have let go of Charlie's hand for an instant when he ran up to the sleeping baby. As we left, my mother apologized profusely, and the baby's mother seemed to have accepted the apology, but my mother was inconsolable. On our way home, I heard my father's voice trying to comfort her, and my mother stating repeatedly, "I can't take this anymore, I can't." I would never forget that moment I saw her sad eyes, one of the few times I ever witnessed my mother cry.

As an adult I once asked my mother about this story. It was our custom to recount the narratives of Charlie's early childhood on Ferris Street, before he had to leave home, the puzzle of his disability reviewed repeatedly, often in the kitchen, during a long afternoon before we made dinner. Although my mother always trusted what I remembered of my childhood, and often asked me to verify events, she denied this incident happened and was upset with me for bringing it up. When I told her I wanted to include it in an essay I was writing about Charlie in that time period, she begged me not to. I didn't. This story was not filed in the lexicon of myths we shared about my brother. This story, one of shattered dreams, would have been too public.

Both my parents have now been dead for decades, and there is no one who can corroborate this scene at the picnic. However true or not this story was, to me it reveals the pain my mother was feeling as the mother of a child who needed so much understanding. Doris Anderson, who loved meeting people from all over the world, who taught the first class for new English speakers at Detroit's International Institute, who, to the delight of school children, wore a black and white pleated skirt with letters of the alphabet, never attended another Sunday picnic again as long as my father worked for the *The Detroit News*. Instead, she encouraged me to go with my father and enjoy the polka dances and accordion music and baklava. I am not sure why Charlie hit that baby, but I can guess. He was used to acting out, using his fists when he couldn't understand or was excited by something, even taking swings at me or my mother unintentionally. In the thrill of seeing a new baby, slapping was the only way he could express his enthusiasm. That is my version of the story, the myth I carry. I think my mother probably would have understood it this way, too, if she'd let herself, but the memory was too painful. I never brought it up again, but when I asked her what she remembered of the time as Charlie's mother, she told me, "Almost every day, I felt like crying. And once I started, I would never stop."

House and Weeds

In an old photograph, a shadow cast by the dark wing of our house almost touches the four of us sitting on the front yard lawn. My mother is reaching for our squirming baby brother, and then for Charlie, scooting farther and farther away. I am off to the side. We are all dressed in sweaters. I must be ten and Charlie eight at the time, weeks before my parents took him to the institution. Our solid brown brick house is set among others in a platted subdivision carved out of county farmland in the 1950s. The stark gable on the house's wooden façade is barn red to the annoyance of neighbors who preferred white trim. When I was very young, before this photograph, and before the floors inside the house were covered in turquoise carpeting, I looked into the light brown grain of the wood and thought I saw bedsheets whipping on a clothesline. The image looked to me like the sound of someone calling my name.

When I was young, too, I told a friend an outrageous story I firmly believed was true about this childhood house, what Gaston Bachelard calls a "human being's first world." My friend, named Penny, lived down the street and loved warbling TV jingles in her cartoon mouse opera voice: "Chock Full of Nuts is that heavenly coffee, heavenly coffee!" Her eyes rolled skyward and her arms floated at her sides as she sang whenever we played. Without luck I'd try to stop her and make her pay attention to me. It was the summer of 1959, when tunes from the musical *Oklahoma* could be heard on the radio. Penny was singing those too, far off in her backyard by the fence where the family's biscuit-colored hounds were penned. I yelled, "Penny, you know what?" but she kept singing to the dogs, ignoring me. "Yesterday, our house was falling down and I stood like this," I showed her, standing with my shoulders thrust up against the wooden fence. "I held up our house all by myself. In Oklahoma!" I think she finally stopped.

What moved me to make up this story, as much as I can remember, was the background noise of our house, a constant, worrying buzz of adult lament—yells, bangs, reprimands, the sounds children recognize, even at a distance as they play. My house was falling down. I was the eldest child in the family, a girl. My job was to hold the house up, with all the strength of my shoulders. My brother Charlie, at two years old, was becoming what was known then as a child hard to manage. Adding to their stress, my mother had lost her mother and my father had lost his father, both within that year. I was attempting to assert myself against this noise, trying to articulate my role in my family's developing narrative, willing my own explanation in the midst of chaos. Bachelard would say I was preserving the work of dreams and daydreams—the rush to protect the childhood house that lives on in the imagination, no matter what age we are.

By the time my brother was four and then five years old, my parents were thrust even deeper into the mystery of his malady, a phase of uncertainty and bewilderment. He was well past the toddler stage, and although he was walking, he was not yet speaking any words. (Within time, with my mother's help, he would gain some language.) He always seemed unhappy—never laughing or giggling like a young child, but crying, kicking, and screaming for hours. The fact of my brother's incapacity to speak or develop must have been the pervading irrational force of my parents' lives. Not one doctor offered any hope, or seemed to have any experience with his symptoms. I can only imagine the pain they felt, not knowing the cause of Charlie's "brain damage" as one doctor's report recorded. They were seeking explanations at a time when there was little information about children like Charlie.

In the 1950s and 1960s, the expectations for mothers were enormous, far beyond human possibility. My mother had a child to take care of who wasn't learning to talk, who screamed when he wanted something, who hummed constantly and preferred to play alone. My memory is that she often became angry with me, yelling when I didn't expect it and punishing me with a few swipes of a belt when I had no idea what I had done. I watched her like the weather, and tried to stay out of her way when the clouds gathered. Once, I stopped in the blacktop center of Ferris Street, struck by the loud voices of mothers from houses on both sides as they yelled at their kids, all at the same time, like a chorus. Even mothers who didn't have kids like Charlie or girls like me lost their tempers, I realized.

Far from her childhood home, my mother may have felt estranged from her family because as gifted as she was teaching other children to talk, she couldn't at first grasp Charlie's disability enough to explain it to them. Charlie's care took up so much of her time when he was little, she couldn't talk on the phone with her sister (a mother of eight kids herself) and she couldn't go back to the work she loved in speech therapy, which she had done up until his birth. She would later teach elementary school, but before that, these were isolating years for her. My father soon fell into the habit of avoiding our family, pressured to take late nights at the newspaper, what he called "working midnights," those shifts beginning at 11:00 p.m. and ending the next day at 7:00 a.m. Also, after my grandfather died, my father carried the responsibility of his mother, my beloved grandmother Helen, who remained an hour and a half north of us in Saginaw.

In spite of her isolation, my mother made friends with another woman, active in her Black community in Mt. Clemens and a member, like my mother, of the League of Women Voters. A few times when my mother had access to our car, she took Charlie and me to her friend's home where we played in the backyard with an older girl in the family while both mothers attended to League business. I had no idea what my mother and her friend were talking about, but likely they were monitoring voting rights, central in the news then and of keen interest to my mother. At home, as we watched scenes on the TV news depicting anti-integration rioters in Little Rock, Arkansas, my mother would tell me about the overt racism, referred to then as segregation, toward Black communities she had witnessed growing up in the South. When she started providing speech correctionist services in Tampa in the late '40s, my mother said, she felt compelled to defy segregation rules and go into Black schools, finding a janitor's closet with just enough room to fit two chairs for the child and herself where they could sit among the mops and brooms.

Mt. Clemens, north of Detroit, was a factory suburb of a factory city. Five miles away was Metropolitan Beach on Lake Saint Clair, not considered a Great Lake, but our lake, the one we school kids counted as number six when we were quizzed. On a clear day you could see across the lake to Canada, and often a fleet of working vessels carrying ore or other cargo through the shipping lane. Evaporation from the lake and nearby Clinton River made the air so damp in summertime you could almost drink it. Also in the air was a peculiar odor, what my father called *rotten eggs*, when he opened the front door on a summer morning, an odor harkening back to the early twentieth century when Mt. Clemens was known for its curative sulfur baths. Our neighborhood, today part of Clinton Township, and not Mt. Clemens proper, was bordered not only by the river but the Hillcrest Country Club where no one we knew golfed. Across the river, to the east, the direction our house faced, was the Mt. Clemens Pottery that sounded a factory whistle as the shifts changed, day and night.

When my brother Charlie and I were young, our half-acre lot had a wild feel to it, especially the backyard. If I stood on a chair and looked out the dining room window facing west at the end of day, I could see the uneven grass and weeds of the yard turn a golden tinge, reflecting the sun's last rays. I loved all the weeds of the backyard—dandelions, thistles and clover. I raced through this resplendence each spring, picking Queen Anne's lace at my knees, inhaling the fresh grass that smelled, as I looked up, like the sky. I knew every inch of the yard and probably could still locate, walking the property line, all the ruts and holes that had once appeared in that flat landscape. Sometimes I would find a scrambling box turtle who'd lost its way to the creek, or an arrowhead or two buried in the yard, firing my imagination with the lives of the Algonquin peoples who had once lived in the area.

Every morning Charlie was a bold streak in cut-off pants, running out to our large backyard as if he possessed it. He would wave his hands and arms as insects buzzed the weeds and birds chattered and squawked. Sam, our curly long-legged Airedale, chased in pursuit of Charlie, barking at his heels as he tried to climb over the chain link fence into the next yard. If Charlie put his foot up on the fence, Sam immediately set his jaws on his rubber sole, shaking it to pry it loose. When Charlie landed back on the ground, Sam ran wide circles through the yard, head bent, hind legs angled low in the wild chase of his bear-hunting ancestors. For almost fifteen minutes, our dog would make these earnest, panting spirals with Charlie a cornered player in his ancient game. Later, Charlie would come back into the house, his lips stained purple from munching the tops of flowering clover he popped into his mouth like candy.

The high, tough grass was hard to mow, and a constant source of conflict between my mother and father. My father, not the outdoorsy type, was happy to let the grass proliferate before taking out the mower and cutting a while until he became bored. Aware of fussy neighbors who already thought we were off-kilter, my mother didn't like to see the weeds thickening, prompting complaints. She was one who ended up hauling the mower out of the garage to finish the job, her nose twitching, Kleenex tucked into the pocket of an old shirt of my father's. I was told to guard Charlie while she carried out the task. Instead, I watched her bend to curl the rope around the gasoline starter, then throw off a slew of curse words each time the lawnmower failed to engage. I thought it was hilarious.

On his days off, my father liked to tease me, pretending I had done something wrong that would lead to punishment. I loved these experiments in being bad. When he headed out the door on an errand, our conversation would go something like:

"Get in the car."

"Where are we going?"

"I'm taking you to jail."

"What did I do wrong?"

"You're bad. You talk too much. Now get in the car."

As we drove, I'd ask him how long I'd be in jail, would he come visit, what would I eat, etc. He rarely gave an answer. We did this dozens of times. Why did I enjoy it so much? I may have been in awe of bad behavior, especially what I'd seen among boys. My brother Charlie's tantrums and screaming were irritating, but also fascinating. I wanted to test the boundaries myself, figure out which rules to obey and which ones I could push to the edge and then ignore. My compulsion to talk about everything I saw or heard defined my existence but my parents seemed intent on making me stop. My brother Charlie was virtually nonverbal, yet much noisier than me. They left him alone, I noticed.

A chore my father happily volunteered to do was burn the trash in a metal barrel with holes on the side that he set out in the backyard. Near the barrel was a crabapple tree, craggy and knotted, the remainder of the yard's old growth in what was once a field. I liked the tree because it was small, a child's height. One Sunday afternoon I was with Dad as he prepared to set the trash ablaze when he asked me, "Cathy, do you know who Abraham was?" I said I'd never heard of him.

"In the Bible, Abraham had a son, Isaac," he continued. "And God tells Abraham that he's going to have to kill his son and throw him into the fire." Why was my father telling me this story? I wonder now if he could have been thinking of Charlie, and the difficult decisions he would need to make about his son's future. Dad flicked a match into the crumpled newspapers, twigs and branches. A fire lit quickly at first, and then died to a low smolder. This was the scariest story I had ever heard.

"Why would God do that?" I asked.

"Because he's God and he's all powerful."

I took this in, thinking of Abraham, a grown man, having to follow instructions from this illogical God he couldn't argue with. I often had to obey commands I didn't understand. I could imagine the terror Abraham must have felt. How easy it was to lose your life in the face of this God.

After a few minutes my father said, "And then, just as Abraham was raising his knife over Isaac an angel appears and tells him he doesn't have to kill his son."

"Oh." Even Abraham, an adult, had to pass a test, I thought. We were both quiet as the papers and twigs flared up, smoke sailing over the crab apple tree.

"This was all a long time ago," my father said.

I considered the story he just told. "Would you ever kill me and throw me into the fire?" I asked.

"No, don't be silly. I wouldn't do that."

"What if I'm bad?"

"Then you go to jail."

Without talking anymore, we tended the fire in the metal barrel by the crabapple tree. Our house, seen from the backyard, looked silent, all the blinds drawn except for the kitchen window where I saw my mother watching Dad and me. In the piles of photographs of our childhood, I've never found one taken of our house on Ferris Street from that angle. Still, I remember this picture of her watching us from the kitchen of our childhood house, and even further in the back of my mind, the house as my mother herself.

NOUNS AND VERBS

It would be a number of years before I would find that startling story from the Old Testament to read on my own. I realized early on the ability to read gave a protective power to anyone in its possession. And I could sense that power would eventually be mine, and not my brother Charlie's. On first learning to read as a child, there was a moment when I felt all the sounds of all the letters fall into place, as if the word were beginning to match the picture, but I'm not sure when. My mother often didn't have time to read to me, and didn't believe children should be rushed. Nonetheless, I picked up anything I could to try to read from what I knew, viewing billboards, cereal cartons and matchbooks with fascination, pondering the strange meaning of signs in front of shops, such as "Tool and Die." As a young child I felt overpowered whenever I met older children who read real, thick books in school. When my parents needed to take Charlie for a week-long evaluation at the hospital at the University of Michigan in Ann Arbor, they placed me in an overnight summer camp. It was after my kindergarten year and I was the youngest child there. I remember telling the camp counselor that I should go home because I hadn't yet, like the other girls, read a book.

About three months into second grade, right after Thanksgiving, my education in words began in earnest. My parents scooped me out of Clinton Valley Elementary, the local public school, and plunked me down in Sister Virginia's class at St. Thecla's, our church's brand-new parish school. Sister Virginia, one of several Felician sisters of Eastern European background, taught by the paddle and the spanking machine located in Sister Superior's office closet. On my first day, I joined fifty other kids in my class as we filed into a large room where the first graders in their cranberry plaid uniforms were singing "Holy God We Praise Thy Name" right beside—I couldn't believe my eyes—a vending machine that offered chocolate milk. In public school there was no such thing as chocolate milk. This was truly a holy moment.

Not too soon after my introduction to St. Thecla's, my father asked me, "Cathy, do you know what a noun is?" I was standing on a chair to grab a loaf of bread from the top of the refrigerator.

"No, I don't," I answered. In the middle of the afternoon I was hungry and wanted to make a peanut butter sandwich.

My father continued, "a noun is a thing, or a person or an animal. You are a noun. So is the dog and the refrigerator." At St. Thecla's I'd just started to learn cursive handwriting and the sounds of vowels. Nouns? This was the first I'd heard of those. I stood on the chair with my hand on the plastic bread wrapper.

"Now, do you know what a verb is?" he asked me.

"No."

"A verb is a word for anything that moves, like the word *drive*." Or something that just is. Is *is* a verb. Do you understand me?"

"I think so."

"Now, tell me, is *eat* a noun or a verb?" he asked. *Eat,* the word uppermost on my mind. I gave the right answer. He was pleased. Once again, I had listened closely and learned something from him. My hunger was almost overwhelming. I grabbed the bread and climbed down from the chair. As I made my sandwich, I thought about this interesting idea—a world divided into things that moved and things that didn't.

At St. Thecla's School, I learned not only the parts of speech, but vowel and consonant sounds and fun rhymes to remember the peculiarities of English pronunciation, such as "When two vowels go a' walking, the first one does the talking." I learned to memorize prayers of contrition, praise and the ones I paid closest attention to: prayers of petition, like the beautiful Memorare with its wild proclamation, "I fly to thee, Oh Virgin of virgins, my Mother! Before thee I stand, sinful and sorrowful!" I learned quickly, for the sake of survival and the promise of chocolate milk. The days were rigorous, starting earlier and ending later than public school, and we were required to do at least two hours of homework—rote memorization not only of prayers, but the orders of angels, names of state capitals, or the longest rivers of the world. The next day we had to be ready to deliver, standing beside our desks when called upon. If we weren't prepared, we could expect to be punished. It was rough going, but I took to the discipline and attention my mother couldn't provide at home as she cared for Charlie. I liked my plaid uniform and plaid book bag. I believed Sister when she told us the devil lurked everywhere we went, like dust—in our classroom, under our beds, or even, as we were reminded in preparation for our first Holy Communion, in the form of blood gushing from our mouths if our teeth nicked the Communion host.

The cadence of church Latin we were taught in that pre-Vatican II world, the Mass with its echo of "Kyrie, Kyrie," caught my ear and stayed with me long after Mass was over. I was also intrigued by the sonic richness of East European and Slavic names in my class at St. Thecla's. My classmates, primarily of Polish, Yugoslavian, German and Italian descent—around one hundred fifty in our grade—had names ending in melodious vowels like Palazzolo, or tingling ski's and sky's like Zielinski or Kwikowsky. These sounds made me think of women with long black hair dancing in vivid colored skirts and blouses. The music of fiddles and concertinas could be heard in those names. My ordinary Scottish name I could associate with no sound: three unaccented syllables, heavy with lazy vowels, the schwa kind. With one of those Eastern European names, you were granted a roomful of laughing uncles and aunts and cousins who danced to polka music, like they did at the community picnics my father took me to. We had no nearby relatives who would visit and celebrate a festival with us. On one of his European reporting trips my father brought me back a Polish national costume, a striped green skirt with a ribbon hem and a velvet vest with sequins. It was pretty but I only wore it for my parents' friends who loved calling me by my Polish name Kasha as they taught me basic phrases in their language.

When my parents decided to purchase my First Holy Communion dress in Hamtramck, a city within the city of Detroit where the same Eastern European immigrant population as the Felician sisters of St. Thecla's worked and lived, Sister Virginia announced to my second-grade class, "Cathy's dress is from Hamtramck." I was delighted to be recognized by Sister Virginia. My first Holy Communion was a special time, the end of May, my birthday, and one week later, at the beginning of June, the birth of a new baby in our family, my youngest brother Bill. He was healthy, pink and fat, and as I learned later from my mother, a trouble-free birth. This time, my parents made sure to choose the local hospital in Mt. Clemens rather than Detroit. I couldn't wait for the school day to end so that I could rush home to see him.

What came into the house, too, were a batch of baby books written by experts of the time, although I don't remember seeing the popular Dr. Spock. These were written for adults, but I devoured them. How to bathe a baby, feed and burp and rock him to sleep were totally fascinating to me. If my father was too rough in the burping, I stepped in to show him the correct way to do it. Charlie was also enchanted by the new baby, and for years insisted on calling him "Baby Bill," a name we all tried to discourage as Bill grew older. All the phases of infant development, especially how a child develops language, intrigued me that summer as I set aside my floppy baby doll named Lydia to help my mother with the new baby, and to also help her even more diligently watch over Charlie.

The Dream Basement

Summer hours Charlie and I would spend in the cool basement of our house on Ferris Street, an underground of porous walls and brown spiders weaving in the low light, their eggs scattered in shadows. Apart from the bright world outside, the basement made no demands of us. Those afternoons we drifted far away from the society of childhood that didn't understand my brother and shunned us both. In that damp basement I entered the mystery of his world, taking in his humming, preverbal language without pressure to understand it or translate it to anyone. My brother circled around and around on his tricycle, much too small for him, while I straddled behind on my new silver bike, too large for me. Here we each found our separate freedom, where our voices could rise and warble without significance. All afternoon we paraded through rivers of dust streaming from high windows, past the slow-moving washer and silent furnace. In this whir and hush, this hoot and bellow, my childhood joined my brother's, our mingling and uncoupling more exaggerated as I tried to live two lives, one bearing witness to his, the other my own.

GREEN CARPET AND HIGH WIRES

One Sunday morning I decided to perform a miracle. Oral Roberts was on television, curing sick members of the audience, asking them to come forward so the Lord could heal their limp, their stutter, their paralysis. Charlie and I were sitting in front of the rabbit-eared television set in the living room, each plopped on our own spot of tweedy carpet worn down to threads and foam rubber backing. I was the oldest, so my circle was a bit larger. Our baby brother was still asleep in the bedroom he shared with me. All through the house were these patches in the carpet, brown threads against a dull green that had been turquoise only a year ago. My father had just come through the front door after working midnights. He was now in bed snoring beside my mother and I knew we would not be making it to church for Mass. As I watched the evangelist walk into the audience invoking the healing powers of God, I got up and ran over to Charlie.

I put my hand on my brother's head, what I thought was the site of his affliction, just as Reverend Roberts laid his hands on the motionless legs of a woman in a wheelchair. I prayed for Charlie to be healed from his temper tantrums and inability to speak. As Reverend Roberts yelled "Heal! Heal!" I stood over my brother, one hand touching his head, the other hand on the television, attempting to will a cure, to direct the healing energy through my body to my brother. After a few minutes, I looked over at my brother still sitting on his threadbare circle to see if any change in him had occurred. Nothing.

When Charlie was a baby and before he showed any signs of disability, my father, according to my mother, made the decision to install carpeting throughout the house. "I was in the basement doing laundry in the middle of the day," my mother recounted. "Your father was home and wouldn't you know, two salesmen knocked on the door with carpet samples." When my mother emerged from the basement, my father announced he had ordered what the salesmen called "wall-to-wall carpeting" for the living room, dining room, and the hallway. Workers arrived the next day and spilled heated glue up and down the bare pine floors, then rolled out the thin turquoise carpet.

Within weeks, the carpet fell apart, down to threads held together like "used toilet paper," said my raw-mouthed father. Eventually we all grew used to the brown patches and the worn path down the hallway.

That Sunday morning on television, the woman in the wheelchair got up and walked as the audience broke into gasps. I looked at my brother Charlie again, still sprawled on his spot, unchanged, the same boy. I tried to cure him one more time, my voice soft so my sleeping parents couldn't hear. Nothing. The Oral Roberts show had come to an end and soon would begin a lineup of kid's shows I would enjoy alone with my brother who was placing colored marbles, one by one, on the carpet. I wondered if I should have prayed harder for a cure, one that would transform him into a little brother who could talk, attend school, and stay calm. In the house, spoken in whispers, was talk of my brother one day living in an institution. I wanted a miracle to prevent that from happening.

There was still no clear name for what was wrong with Charlie. Paradoxically, he passed all nonverbal intelligence tests with flying colors, and could hum a tune, my mother claimed, perhaps too confidently, in perfect pitch. One day, when he was six, about the time of the University of Michigan's murky diagnosis of mental illness and mental retardation, my mother took him to meet Mrs. Diamond, the teacher I had dearly loved in kindergarten, to see if he could be admitted to her class. That afternoon when I got home my mother sadly reported, "Charlie won't be going to school. He kicked Mrs. Diamond." I remember feeling mortified. A few years earlier when I was still attending public school, Mrs. Diamond had once come up to me on the playground and taken me into her arms, saying, "Cathy I just wanted to hug you." This had puzzled me. Now I think Mrs. Diamond must have known all along about my brother when I was in her kindergarten class. She probably was trying to understand our family in ways I didn't even realize.

My brother and I didn't have other children over to play because my friends would leave in a panic over Charlie's screaming and kicking outbursts, so much of the time Charlie and I played alone in our own separate orbits. As that Sunday morning turned into the afternoon, I watched a show where girls my age tried their skills walking across a thick tightrope. The mastery of balance and concentration combined to defeat fear enraptured me. I searched for two chairs and spare rope to try out my own tightrope walk, but couldn't find them. Like the other times I'd practiced tap dancing on the bathroom tile to replicate the sound of tap, brush, tap, I would need to improvise. I went to the kitchen closet and found my mother's broom and laid it down on the worn carpeting. Carefully, one foot in front of the other, arms high for balance, I edged across the broomstick, imagining a sea of faces who watched my slow, beautiful traverse across the big tent to the sound of drums and cymbals. I was brave, I was heroic. Once I reached the bristles of the silly broom, the magic vanished and I realized I'd just walked on a thirty-six-inch broomstick laid down on battered carpet. Charlie showed no interest.

Within the next few years, I would question the singular direction of prayer I had been taught at St. Thecla's—this one-sided monologue that supposed a hidden, powerful, and silent audience. Around our house, my parents displayed the familiar touchstones of Catholic faith—crucifix in the hallway, small bust of the Virgin Mary in the bedroom. My father, whose mother was Irish-Canadian and fervently Catholic, gave me a three-inch carved statue of St. Patrick that I still treasure. On the wall of my grandmother's small apartment in Saginaw were portraits of both John F. Kennedy and Pope John the Twenty-third. However, our living room walls were covered by expressions of faith gathered from the local ethnicities of our region—Polish, Slav, Czech and Eastern Orthodox. In Hamtramck my father had purchased a stunning portrait of Our Lady of Czestochowa, known by Poles as the Black Madonna. And on an opposite wall was the black-and-white portrait of an Eastern Orthodox priest, Metropolitan Sheptytsky who was both a mystic and heroic leader in Eastern Europe during World War II.

For years I have wondered why they hung these portraits—icons, really, these testaments of faith—when they never talked to me directly about religion. We didn't say the rosary together, gathered in front of a statue of the Virgin Mary, like many other families in St. Thecla's parish. My mother often declined to attend Mass on Sundays. These portraits hung in our home as a reminder, I've concluded, of the potential for devotion, but not necessarily its fulfillment. To believe in miracles is to believe in a before and an after—before a time of suffering and after, liberation from that suffering. The hope for a miracle, that long middle swath of time we all dwell in, becomes part of the experience. It can last a lifetime. These icons were their hope over many years for a miracle, not a symbol of their belief in one.

Eventually I would give up praying for a cure for Charlie's disability. Instead, I learned the inner bargain of prayer: a fervent request wrapped in the reality that it may or may not be granted. Today I still submit private pleas, I am a little embarrassed to admit, pushing my desire to shape an image of what I need. Like the urge toward prayer is the compulsion to write poems, another practice I've kept, both accomplished as the motion of two hands set to a task. I'm always surprised when either a poem or a prayer seems to emerge out of nowhere.

That Sunday when I tried to cure my brother by placing my hands on his head, those half-spoken prayers for a miracle were not answered, yet I felt the words begin to reshape my understanding, like a poem repeated over and over. A cure at the place where I had laid my hands on my brother would be impossible, yet another change might occur some distance in the future, a different kind of healing. It would probably begin with the acceptance of my brother Charlie for who he was and not as I wanted him to be. This would take a long time.

KITCHEN TABLE

When I entered fourth grade, my mother became my English teacher at St. Thecla's. She was one of three teachers who taught us rotating subjects in math, English and religion. My mother held forth in her own homeroom of fifty children, and then each day taught an hour of English to my class and another class, a total of one hundred fifty children. Over the three years she taught there, she became very popular, teaching us to diagram sentences and write business letters to tourist boards of various states, requesting pamphlets. When the question came up, my mother told her class that yes, after our pets die, they go to heaven, a direct contradiction to Catholic teaching. She was always cool toward me, not wanting to show any favoritism. She insisted I call her Mrs. Anderson, but I found that impossible and kept my mouth shut. Every morning I was the first one up at home, making breakfast for myself and packing my lunch. I headed to catch the early school bus while Mom caught a ride to St. Thecla's from Dad.

Charlie stayed at home, still not able to attend any public or private school. While my mother was working at St. Thecla's, Ollie Nichols took care of him and our little brother. Ollie came from a German immigrant family and knew how to make applesauce from the green apples under our backyard tree. She wore sleeveless housedresses all through the year with black oxfords and white anklets. My mother chose Ollie because she had trained as a practical nurse, someone who could take care of Charlie if an emergency occurred. She soon was able to make Charlie sit still and scribble with crayons at the kitchen table as she cleaned. My mother marveled at Ollie's capacity to calm Charlie down, help him adjust to a daily routine. Ollie accomplished this because she was used to working in defined pockets of time throughout the day. Whenever the pottery factory whistle blew in the middle of her housework, I remember how she'd announce to my brothers and me, "Hear that break whistle? It's time for Ollie to sit down and cool off."

I was never sure if she liked me as I didn't take to housework with the industry she expected in an older sister. She often called me "girl," and insisted I vacuum my bedroom along with other cleaning duties. When I came home from school one afternoon, instead of making me put down everything to clean my room, she told me, "Look what I showed your little brothers." She pulled out a picture of a twenty-year-old woman wearing a kerchief and sitting on the seat of a tractor. It was Ollie, unmistakably. Bill loved it. I'm not sure what Charlie thought of Ollie's photograph. Sometimes he showed an avid interest in pictures of people he knew, or he may have enjoyed the big wheels and the red engine, with Ollie sitting high up in the seat ready to steer it. I didn't ask him. Instead, I sat down and picked up one of his crayons to demonstrate how to draw a sunflower with a dark center and bright orange petals. My drawing was literal, like any nine- or ten-year-old's. He ignored me. Charlie preferred to color in a random fashion, choosing different crayons and zigzagging up and down the page. He didn't care about learning how to draw a real flower, I thought. To me, his crayon sketches were formless, incoherent. They wielded no mastery and that scared me, causing a swell of anger inside. My brother was going nowhere. I felt bored sitting with him.

Each day I was becoming more aware of the differences between Charlie and me, sensing both my good luck not to be born with his disability, as well as that emotion's flip side—an eerie, almost throbbing fear. Did my teachers, classmates and neighbors view me as having a difference, hidden somewhere, like my brother? Carrying that fear meant I tried to be extra smart and careful not to make mistakes. I was the eldest, and the burden of how my family appeared to others fell on my shoulders. I couldn't imagine what would happen to this disabled brother of mine who could not sit still in a classroom. He didn't recognize the sounds of letters, and scribbled like a two-year-old at the age of seven. These vulnerabilities were frightening to witness. One Sunday morning, my father had cooked bacon and eggs for all of us. After stuffing a slice of bacon into his mouth and smearing eggs on the plate with his fingers, Charlie squealed, then slouched down to the floor and wiped his dirty hands on his head. My father asked me to finish up the food he had left. I refused vehemently, shouting that if I ever ate anything already tasted by him, I would instantly turn into "a Charlie."

Charlie was sometimes calm when he played at home, but there were still very few public places he could tolerate. Eventually, my parents discovered that he became unusually tranquil in grocery stores, riding on the back of the cart my father would push. To give my mother a break, my father would take us to the local I.G.A. store in downtown Mt. Clemens. On entering, I would speed to the magazine rack in another aisle, only stopping to view the butcher's display of hog parts—tails, snouts, feet, and ears, with their bristly hairs and tough skin. After that long glance, I was lost in a *Ripley's Believe It or Not!* paperback, reading how a meteorite hit a ship, not once but fourteen times, believe it or not. My father would sail by with Charlie, telling me to hurry up. Charlie had already picked out the Lucky Charms and Chex, the Campbell's mushroom soup and Wonder Bread, all neatly stacked in the cart. When we got home, he rushed to put away all the groceries. He recognized immediately where everything went by the colors and labels, including the countless blue cans of dog food for Sam, almost as if he were reading by sight. He even put a five-pound bag of sugar—the standard size back then—in the front closet to the surprise of my mother who assumed he didn't know where she hid it. She kept it there because once he had eaten the whole bag.

I was the fortunate daughter. Unlike Charlie, I was mastering sentences and writing paragraphs. I was reading books about unbelievable facts and crazy inventions, Roman Catholic saints and the aviatrix Amelia Earhart. One evening when my father was home, he called me to his side as he held a newspaper and a mirror on his lap. He tilted the mirror to the page and told me to first read the large black letters of the headlines and then the smaller words of the article, all in reverse. I gained speed as I read with growing ease, delighted by the novelty. I knew this was another one of Dad's tests of my comprehension, checking in to make sure I was still the smart kid in the family. He had been reading like this all day at work, Dad explained, proofreading the letterpress pages. I was doing the same kind of work, as good as anyone at *The Detroit News*, he told me. I jumped off his lap, happy my father was happy.

THE FOURTH OF JULY

I remember how clouds clustered above Lake Saint Clair overnight until morning when they hung like a metal shelf over the landscape. One particular Fourth of July, it rained all morning, the grass swollen green until afternoon when the sun finally came out. A holiday in the middle of the week, a break in routine, was always hard for Charlie. Every family in our neighborhood welcomed the day off, each home guarded by a family Ford or Dodge in a driveway lined with white rocks. Up and down the street, the smell of smoke wafted from outdoor grills. Since Christmas Charlie had been asking for things in an odd, echo-patterned language: want cookie? want milk? want that pop? Even though it was summer, he could be heard singing "Rudolph the Red-Nosed Reindeer" as he looped around and around the front of the garage on his small red tricycle. I remember that Mom and Dad seemed cheered by his singing, anticipating the moment when he would begin to talk more fluently, perhaps answer a question using the word "I." Mom lit a sparkler, hoping to enchant him, but he ran away. Older boys from the next block were popping firecrackers. The noise was excruciating for him, even though it seemed far away to us. He screamed as he ran from the backyard into the house, his hands tightly covering his ears and his legs scissoring up and down. We couldn't tell if he felt pain or unbearable terror. I watched Mom take my brother into her arms and roll him up in a blanket head to toe, "like a hot dog," I said. She laid him down on their large double bed, where he became calm for the first time in hours, his penny-brown eyes closed, his head a chestnut whorl against the nap of the blanket.

SOUTH JEFFERSON STREET

"You don't love Charlie!" I yelled at my father one Saturday morning.
I felt like he had it coming. He had just lost his temper over another thing
Charlie had done accidentally, dumping sugar which he craved irresistibly,
and spreading it all over the floor. Dad was red-faced, standing in his bathrobe
with a cup of coffee, his slippers making a tacky sound. He called Charlie
"simple," which upset me. It meant the same thing as the word "retard," one
I knew from chants I heard at school directed at anyone who didn't kick a
ball fast enough, or missed an obvious punchline to a joke. I was on guard if
any one of those kids saw Charlie and called him names, and I wouldn't let
my father get away with it either. He immediately froze and didn't respond
to me. He was probably tired after working the night before and just wanted
sugar for his coffee. My accusation was cruel, but I could tell in an instant
when a child was loved and when he or she wasn't. I knew this because my
grandmother Helen, my father's mother, a widow who worked as a substitute
kindergarten teacher in Saginaw, never ceased to show me that I was loved
unconditionally.

Charlie was to inherit a bag of shiny silver dollars from our grandfather,
but I received an abundance of care from this grandmother who combed her
fingers through my hair and knelt with me to say my prayers. I saw her only at
Christmas, and for a number of weeks in the summer at her home in Saginaw,
but it was enough tenderness to carry me through childhood. I wish she had
loved Charlie in the same way, but he may have been too difficult for her to
understand. When he didn't respond to her hugs or prompts to sing "You
Are My Sunshine," she'd frown, then pull back in bewilderment, and I think,
hurt. She embraced the dominant myth in our family that something terribly
wrong had happened at Charlie's birth. She avoided the phrase "mentally
retarded" when discussions about him came up, and she never asked my
parents any questions. She certainly must have picked up on my father's
quick irritation with Charlie, but she never rose to his defense. Instead, she
lavished her attention on me, something I needed, she claimed, referring to

the bruises Charlie left on my shins from his swift kicks in hard-soled shoes.

My grandmother's house was a first-floor one-bedroom apartment within a two-story Queen Anne in an old neighborhood not far from downtown on South Jefferson Street. The house must have been built in the 1880s and was located next to a tall gray mansion that was the city's Historical Society where documents of its lumber baron history were stored. Down the driveway was a carriage house that drew me in as most old things did. It was impossible to open the large double doors, so instead I backed away to get a running start, and then ran toward the narrow windows of the doors, leaping up repeatedly to see what was inside. With each jump, I took in the disarray of abandoned buggies and wheels and lanterns from another century. There were no horses, or stable boys brushing them down, but this was the most exciting thing I had ever seen. Catching my breath, I ran back up the steps to unlock the heavy door and sped through the vestibule that smelled like wet silk until I reached my grandmother's apartment and announced what I'd just discovered.

My grandmother wanted me running in and out of her apartment because she was lonely for company during the summer when she wasn't teaching. Her husband, my grandfather Andy, had died a few years earlier from a heart attack in the green chair in the front of the television set, his fingers reaching too late for the nitroglycerin tablets buried in his pocket. He was an agricultural chemist, born Arnold Plummer (my grandmother always called him Andy) in Warrensburg, Missouri, and educated as a scholarship student in the early 1900s at the Pratt Institute in New York. He invented a process to convert sugar beets, known to taste like a potato with sugar sprinkled on it, into liquid sugar. My grandfather received no remuneration for the patent, owned by the Pioneer Sugar Company in Saginaw. He never bought a house for his family, only the white Plymouth both grandparents drove. My grandmother told me that he had no head for business, but simply wanted to work in his lab "and patch up burns for the men in the sugar factory." He would have been following his own father, a horse-and-buggy doctor in late nineteenth century Warrensburg. Even though my grandfather died when I was five, I remembered him, legs stretched out on our couch on Ferris Street, when he came to visit. I liked to tap on the top of his head with its spare hairs that looked like a stringed instrument. "What happened to your hair?" I asked him. "Your grandmother pulled it all out!" he told me.

The love I received from my grandmother was shown not only in her care for me, but her trust in my sense of the world. Quite a gift for a child to receive—to be believed by an adult. Once again, I was the lucky kid in the family. She listened to me and I listened to her, something Charlie was not able to do. I would stay those summers with her from the time I was seven until I turned thirteen. When I first came to visit, she had a double bed that took up most of the living room in the small apartment. It had been Andy's and I slept in it under the powder blue eiderdown she saved from the Ontario winters she knew as a child. Eventually she got rid of the bed and I slept on a natty sofa, what she called "the davenport," under a picture of her, the youngest child in the family, encircled by her seven brothers and sisters. During the night, those brothers and sisters floated above me in their best church clothes, the girls decked out in lace, the boys with combed hair and white ties. In the early morning, one of them would settle in my grandmother's easy chair to wait for light to come through the tall windows before disappearing from the living room.

In the morning when I reported all of this to my grandmother, she listened, nodding. Then she changed the topic to one of her dreams, perhaps about a peevish friend of hers—someone who made a comment about her dress, or a hand she played in the bridge tournament we attended in Bay City the night before. While she played bridge, I would flip through *Superman* comic books and *Life Magazine*, sprawled on a leatherette couch in the hotel lobby. At breaktime, I would come out to the tournament tables to scoop up peanuts and get a good look at everyone. On mornings following a tournament, she loved talking about the event with me, getting my opinion of the people we met. It would be about 10:00 a.m. and she would still be in her pajamas and robe. As the morning wore on, out of the blue she might ask, "Cathy, do you know I am a psychologist?" enunciating the last word with grandeur. She would point to a large volume on the bookshelf titled something like *The Family Dictionary of Psychology* and ask me to take it down for her. For a few minutes, she'd read aloud from this book, still talking about her dream, or the puzzling details of her bridge friends. I'd put the book back eventually, next to her brass trophy showing a hand of cards and another title with a gold-embossed spine that always intrigued me, *Parnell's Speeches from the Dock*. When I asked her about this book, she told me it contained the most beautiful speeches ever written, and by an Irishman, of course, because no one could write better than the Irish.

Each morning we made breakfast together in the kitchen built into an eave, the ceiling just high enough to fit her frame and mine. As we made tea and toast with grape jelly, she chattered about the places we'd go that morning, perhaps to see her friend Rose Mudd, whose husband's grandfather was the man who treated John Wilkes Booth on the run after assassinating Abraham Lincoln. Mr. Mudd sent a Christmas card every year of himself in the dank prison cell his grandfather was condemned to for "simply doing his duty as a doctor in treating a wounded man." Visiting Kresge's was also on our list, mainly to watch people and look at the parakeets among the ladies' bras and dishes. I once saw a tall shelf lined with plastic dolls for Black children, sheathed in shiny cellophane wrap, like the dolls for white girls, but only in a tawny brown color. Except for the daughter of my mother's friend from the League of Women Voters, my understanding of Black children was limited to the few glimpses on Detroit television early on Sunday mornings, or driving through my grandmother's neighborhood. No Black people at the time lived in my neighborhood in Mt. Clemens. I was curious about these dolls and thought of asking for one. I knew my curiosity would have been discouraged and so I kept quiet.

My grandmother always dressed in pearls and high heels, even for these ordinary trips downtown or to see friends. Before we left, she would snap a red headband on my head to keep the bangs out of my eyes. Every summer she bought me a new set to wear in Saginaw and told me to wear them at home, too. She said to never shirk from doing something I wanted, peppering that advice with stories of her own childhood heroics up in a backyard tree, announcing her intention to fly. Wearing a headband was really not one of the things I wanted to do, and I had no intention of flying out of a tree. I took note, though, in how she escaped from a nun about to hammer her knuckles with a ruler. This I could see myself doing. She must have recognized a similar spark of rebellion in me. When I was introduced to her friends, she often said, "And this is my granddaughter, who's afraid of nothing!"

On Sundays, after Mass, we always lit a candle by the statue of St. Joseph, the guardian of families, and the saint who would protect Charlie, my grandmother would tell me. This is how I knew she loved him, and how I comprehended, from an early age, that something was seriously wrong with my brother that no adult could describe.

As a kindergarten teacher, my grandmother played piano even though she never owned one. She still sang tunes from Gilbert and Sullivan as she dipped her head in earnest, songs that Charlie, who loved music, never stayed around for. I probably didn't pay any attention either, thinking this music was suited only for little children. She told me often that as a child she danced, sang and acted in her hometown of Ingersoll, Ontario, where she had been one of the stars of the town's production of *H.M.S. Pinafore*, playing the role of Buttercup. A talent scout from New York had even talked to her father about a career in acting, playing roles in theaters along the east coast. My grandmother said he wouldn't permit her to leave home.

What did happen next in her life at the age of twelve or thirteen I didn't learn from her but from my mother. Into the first decade of the 1900s, Ingersoll was battling a severe tuberculosis outbreak and my grandmother's sister Ethel almost didn't survive it. Their parents decided to send both Helen and Ethel, only a few years apart in age, to Denver where my great-grandfather's sister, a nun, worked as a pharmacist for what must have been a sanatorium treating tuberculosis patients. A school for girls was also located there, Loretto Heights Academy, where this aunt arranged for the girls to attend. My great-grandfather, a one-legged station master for the Canadian Pacific Railroad, procured cheap tickets for their passage. In the story my mother told, the parents sent the girls together because they didn't want them to be lonely. My mother said my grandmother would recall, when she talked of her days at Loretto, of waking one night to hear a girl weeping on top of her trunk in the dormitory. My mother always thought my grandmother may have been that girl, but never admitted it.

From my mother's telling of this story, it's clear she tried to understand her mother-in-law Helen, but the truth was she didn't like her. I've always remembered my mother's account of my grandmother's early life as another story of how, in our family, a child once again had to leave the home they'd always known. About my grandmother, my mother guessed that after she was put on the train out of Ingersoll, she never matured completely to become a responsible adult, or act like a maternal figure "who made cookies, instead of going to bridge tournaments and sleeping until ten every morning." My mother faulted her for not trying to help with Charlie when he was a child, and for leaning on my father constantly. Most likely my grandmother didn't offer to help with Charlie because she was afraid of doing the wrong thing. She leaned on my father because he was her only child, and after the death of her husband, her closest relative. When my father was in the war, and out of touch for months, my grandmother apparently became mentally unstable with grief and had to be medicated. This, too, could be another family story of a boy lost from his mother.

Everyone else adored my grandmother. She seemed to be known by all the families in Saginaw as we walked down the street together. She had a child's view of the world, amplified by her diminutive stature and good humor. A child could be easily enchanted by her attention and the fact that Charlie never fell under her spell didn't stop her from trying or dampen her confidence with children. Early on when I came to visit, she introduced me to kids she knew who lived on the court, a series of row houses on South Jefferson connected by a short alley to the gravel lot behind the tall Queen Anne. I spent many afternoons playing board games or running through the neighborhood with Susie, Brian or Donnie. On long summer nights when the sun didn't set until late that far north, you could hear the sonorous echoes of children's voices, so different from the flattened cacophony of my neighborhood on Ferris Street. Sounds climbed up the house eaves, over the tall old beeches and oaks. In summer, too, you could hear pigeons cooing in the morning, offset by the shrieks of squirrels in the afternoon.

The houses on the court and the house my grandmother lived in were owned by the same detested landlord. Everyone, including my grandmother, complained about the lack of heat and high rent. Directly behind us, edging the gravel parking lot, was a hill of abandoned tires and junk that sloped down to the landlord's small office building. One summer, Brian and his sister Susie and I were walking across the logs laid out in the parking lot when both stopped and proudly pointed out the side of the landlord's building covered in brown streaks. Just the week before I'd come to visit my grandmother, they had egged the building. I was sorry to have missed that moment and amazed they never got in trouble.

Another sound that stayed afloat from summer to summer over my grandmother's Saginaw neighborhood was the low, soft murmur of a human voice. It changed throughout the day, becoming first a question, and then sometimes a full-blown laugh, drifting from the house across the street. I heard it as I played on the front porch of the house with its filigreed railing. When I followed the sound, I'd see a man sitting on a porch swing, directly across from me. I may have waved, and he may have waved back. From a distance he looked chubby, with dark hair. He smiled, briefly, as if he were shy. Unusual, I thought, a shy grown-up. I sat on the porch and watched him for a while before becoming bored and going inside. When I asked my grandmother who he was the first time I saw him, she said, "What a pity. Their son, such a big man living at home." I wondered if she had ever spoken with him, and if he knew her the way the kids on the court did. She didn't explain why she had said that, but I realized she meant he would never grow up. He had something hard to describe, the same thing that was wrong with Charlie. When we pulled out of the driveway on one of our trips downtown, my grandmother shook her head again as she looked toward the porch where he lived. She never told me his name.

PORTRAIT OF A BOY AND BEETLE

With one ear to the ground, I think it may have been possible to hear ghosts of fallen oaks, the land once wild, now flattened for the upright brick house and two-car garage on Ferris Street. For years, beetle larvae, curled like commas, had gestated inside the oak walls of the garage until one warm morning a stag beetle woke to maturity where it shouldn't be, dropped behind a gasoline can. There it began a slow journey to find tree sap and rotting apples. At the same time, Charlie ran to the garage searching for marbles and smooth pebbles, things below his feet. While he lay on his stomach, the stag beetle crossed the concrete floor into the gritty cave of his palm. The boy who never spoke then stroked the beetle's black iridescent thorax and red mahogany wings. He lightly touched the mandibles, projecting like miniature deer antlers in the slatted light. His eyes followed the beetle's waving antennae and he stared at it as if the beetle were his first friend in kindergarten. When our mother asked to see what he'd found, he wouldn't show her and ran to a corner of the garage, cupping the beetle in his hands, his hands close to his heart. For a few hours there was comfort in this sadness, as if by connecting to a small insect he might come closer to us—mother, father, little brother and me. By noon, the beetle, caged too long in the prison of Charlie's fingers, revolted and bit him. Charlie wailed and wailed. Then he stopped and turned inward again like the quiet ghost of an oak tree.

II
HE WOULD TELL US IF HE COULD

Beginning To Speak

My brother Charlie's journey toward speech, so valued by my family, was a long one. By the age of three, my mother and father recalled, Charlie had uttered only one nonsensical sound: "gwee." My mother had substantial professional experience training children with disabilities to speak, yet nothing prepared her for the challenge of her own son. To teach Charlie, my mother gathered her collection of what was known as the tools of a speech correctionist, described in her 1919 *Manual of Exercises for the Correction of Speech Disorders*: flags, feathers, candles, bags, plastic rings for soap bubbles, whistles, popsicle sticks, pinwheels, handbells. To me the most fascinating of all were the hand puppets she created. She put all of these to use in her attempt to encourage Charlie's speech, a deeply physical process requiring a mastery of breath the manual explained in words that would never duplicate the reality of my brother's struggle: "The air must make no noise in going in or coming out. It should be inhaled and exhaled without straining, the body being perfectly relaxed. Before beginning to speak we must inhale quickly and deeply with the mouth slightly open. We speak on the outgoing breath." Charlie showed no interest in this complicated feat. His hearing had tested normal and he had no anatomical barriers to speech such as a cleft palate, unlike other children my mother had taught. What was making it impossible for him to speak?

Our house was filled with the varying sounds and expressions of language, ample background, one would think, for a child learning to speak. When they could, my parents invited friends of theirs from the large Eastern European community to our home in Mt. Clemens. I often fell asleep to the sound of accented English and laughter ringing through the house. The next morning, I would find the once energetic guest who had swept me up in his burly arms the night before now snoring on our living room couch. My father was known for his unique ability to plumb stories and anecdotes from immigrants with even the most basic English, picking up words from their language as he conversed. He often consulted dictionaries he bought in a number of the main languages of the communities of Detroit at the time: Polish, Czech, and Romanian. He told me that he could read most newspapers published in those languages with the help of a dictionary; he never claimed fluency, just curiosity.

My father's capacity for comprehension wasn't limited to new speakers of English. My friend Janice who lived down the street was deaf. She wore hearing aids and could read lips. Most of the time we played active games that didn't require a story line, such as golf swings or bouncing on a pogo stick. Playing with her I needed a minute or so to comprehend what she was telling me and even my mother, trained to work with children who were deaf, had trouble understanding her. But if my father answered the door when she came by the house, he would engage her in what seemed like a chatty exchange about her day at school, the weather, and what she liked to play. He then would report back to me, seeming to understand everything she had said.

The main way a child learns to talk is by interacting with his or her mother, father, and other family members who repeat the names of things and turn the child's attention to new experiences, enriching the hours they spend together with songs, rhymes and other games that have a strong social component. Usually, effortlessly, the child picks up the sounds of words through imitation and begins to construct rudimentary language from mutually shared experiences. For a child with autistic traits, like my brother, social interaction was minimal. He did not respond easily to other children and often ignored me and my father although he was intrigued by our new baby brother Bill from a distance. He connected with our mother more directly, but often resisted her affection and attention. Charlie could spend hours rocking in a small rocking chair of his, waving his fingers, or flicking a light switch on and off. He was almost four before he learned how to use the toilet on his own. The University of Michigan medical community where my parents sought help had no theory or explanation for why he couldn't respond to his mother's embracing smile or father's teasing laughter.

My parents felt they had no choice but to keep trying everything they could think of to teach Charlie to talk. My mother put away her speech correction manuals and began observing him even more closely in her attempt to understand his growing mind. In a letter to me, she described this period: "Some of the circumstances of the isolation that characterized my experiences actually provided more one-on-one time to work with him." Many of the techniques my mother conjured to sustain his attention and spark his verbal response pre-dated what has become standard practice for working with non-verbal children with autism. Some things worked, others didn't. To help him shape words from sounds, she taught him to spin a pinwheel by blowing on it as he watched the colors swirl. The hot dog blanket roll I saw her use to soothe him, something she thought of out the blue, has become a practice used now by many parents to calm their distressed children. She absorbed any bit of insight she could pick up from a neighbor or observant friend who seemed trustworthy and interested, even the Avon lady or a store clerk, who knew about children and might offer an idea about how to get him to talk. I remember her making a new friend—a mother with a child with Down Syndrome—and inviting the mother and her son over to our house. After they were gone, she turned to me and said, "If only Charlie could talk like that little boy."

My mother once constructed a puppet theater from cardboard and an old bookshelf. She sewed buttons for eyes and embroidered a mouth on a pair of my father's old socks. Her idea, I think, was to spark Charlie's attention to the babbling sock so that he would begin to imitate words. She must have guessed that he would be enchanted by her fast-moving, quick-talking puppet by once watching him respond, ever so slightly, to puppets on children's television. She wanted to train him to articulate more than the sound "gwee." In the kitchen, she held a short performance that I enjoyed but Charlie ignored, running out of the room. When I kept asking her questions she refused to answer, maintaining her puppet role, I too became bored and left the kitchen. The puppet theater was relegated to the garage, never used again. The mystery remained: what drew Charlie's attention and kept it? Why did he respond to some colors, sounds, and voices, but not to others?

My mother's claim that Charlie scored high on the nonverbal part of an intelligence test when he was tested by the school system to see if he could enter kindergarten in the future, may be hard to prove, but I've always believed her. I have no idea which tests were used then. I assume they were primarily visual, matching shapes and colors. Those tests seemed to have complicated my parents' understanding of what he knew, how he learned it, and how to get him ready for schooling. She also told me that at the age of four, he was copying numbers and letters. It's unlikely that he was grasping their meaning at that age but he was learning how to sit still at a desk and take directions. And after sitting too long, he would get up, like any child, and continue his day in constant motion—running, bellowing, jumping.

When Charlie was about five years old, my mother noticed a break-through. Charlie was humming Christmas carols—without the words, but in tune. He had always been mesmerized by our mother's singing, watching her mouth, and then trying to follow the tune by carrying it himself. He liked the repetitive cycles of a song, and was fascinated by the 45 rpm records turning under the needle of our tiny red and white record player. My mother had a hunch that if his love of music, lights, and pictures could be brought together, he might pronounce some words. From a catalog, she bought a small multi-sided mirror shaped like a prism and constructed to look like a circus tent with a red flag on top. Ready for playing, you placed the mirror in the middle of a record decorated with cartoon figures and images. As the record spun around, the multi-sided mirror reflected the pictures cast from below—snowmen dancing, sleigh bells ringing. Soon, Charlie was singing, "Rudolph the Red-nosed Reindeer." The words were a bit hard to understand, but he seemed to know them all, an amazing feat! Within time, he was making tentative, but real requests for candy or to play outside, a major breakthrough that made us hope for more. My parents felt an inkling of success, yet not relief. He wasn't asking questions or engaging in a conversation. He still seemed easily frustrated when his routines were changed.

Knowing he liked colors and loved certain foods, my mother made marzipan candy molded into individual fruits and vegetables he could point to and name. Where she got the recipe, I have no idea; it was not in any of her cookbooks. She must have bought the almond paste from the same catalog where she found the circus mirror for the record player. She'd mix a cup of almond paste with two cups of confectioner's sugar and one-fourth of a cup of corn syrup, blending it all together until it became the consistency of play dough. She took food coloring and added it to various pieces, molding potatoes and carrots, rolling balls of marzipan over a cheese grater to create an orange, creasing one at the top to make a cherry. She'd set them in front of Charlie on the kitchen table. He was mesmerized. She encouraged him to name the particular fruits and vegetables and the colors. He named them all correctly and popped each one in his mouth.

Around the time Charlie was gaining spoken language, he also revealed an intense interest in the magic of electricity. He was fascinated by electric lights, and intensely curious about light switches and outlets, including the fuse box in the basement that controlled the lights' on/off flashing brilliance. I believe his perception of color was far more intense than the average person's, but that, of course, is only my guess. Any time of the year he enjoyed a display of neon lights, car lights, even porch lights. During the holiday season, we would bundle up at night and take him to gaze at the myriad of green, red and white Christmas lights, a treat we knew he loved by how quiet he became, staring and staring with a big smile on his face as my mother drove through the neighborhood.

By the seriousness with which he played it was clear he was learning, on his own, how exciting aspects of the physical world worked. My mother once showed him a catalogue of Christmas decorations, pointing out the bold colored lights he loved. He ripped out that page immediately and ran off. A day or so later she found the page stuck—apparently by gum or spit—on the fuse box in the basement. I have no idea what he meant, but I like to think he was trying to tell us that he understood the abstract meaning of a picture, how representation correlates with the real thing. He was telling us: *Yes, I do understand this symbol.* What I like most was his passionate intensity. No middle road for Charlie—get down to the basement, lick that page and mash it to the fuse box controlling all light and dark. Like any child, he was probing, with keen interest, a part of the world that fascinated him.

On more than one occasion Charlie would be driven to test this new-found power of electricity with his own hands. We were at the home of friends my father knew from work. It was probably a winter evening, the adults gathered in the living room, enjoying after-dinner conversation. I was playing with one of the girls in her room, and Charlie was downstairs in the basement with a few other kids. All of a sudden, the lights went out. Before the kids could run upstairs to report what happened, my parents had already turned to their hosts and explained carefully that Charlie must have found the fuse box, opened it, and switched off the power.

The most legendary story of all from Charlie's electricity period was the time my mother gave him some metallic thread. She watched him painstakingly unroll it along the baseboard of his bedroom floor, wrap it around a doorknob and then run it up the television antenna in the living room. He would then go flick on the light switch in his room and rush back to the television set to see if a picture came on. My mother let him play, and looked in every once in a while, noticing how he went back and forth with the metal thread, pulling it out to get it perfectly aligned, correcting what he thought were mistakes. In the afternoon a telephone repair man appeared at our door, reporting an outage in phone service at a number of homes on Ferris

Street. My mother and the repair man traced Charlie's carefully laid thread from the television in the living room, through the hallway, and into his bedroom. Apparently, he had wrapped the metal thread around a telephone jack, shorted the cable, and knocked out all the phones in the neighborhood!

In his book *How We Learn,* neurologist Stanislas Dehaene notes that a child's brain craves difficulty. A child tries new activities and then makes mistakes, and with each mistake, begins to learn in a loop called error feedback. This seems like an apt description of Charlie's experiments with electricity, and what he was trying to figure out. Dehaene refers to studies on babies at play by American researcher Lisa Feigensen, who endeavored to prove, in his words, that "whenever children perceive an event as impossible or improbable, learning is triggered." Elsewhere in his book, Dehaene emphasizes the critical role curiosity plays in brain development and learning: "For children to be curious, they need to be aware of what they do not yet know." This higher-order cognition, or "metacognition" constantly "supervises our learning, evaluating what we know and don't know." My brother, in these scenes, possessed the metacognition of any naturally curious boy. He was teaching himself about the world even though he possessed little spoken language.

In Dehaene's book, there is a fascinating photograph of a thick dendritic tree of the six-year-old brain with looping swirls and dots that resemble an electrical current. When I saw it, I wondered, could it be possible that my brother, in his play, was intuiting the neuronal tree pattern of his own brain development? Because Charlie couldn't describe his excitement or ask us questions, and became distressed by so many ordinary things, my family often assumed his mind was chaotic and disorganized. That was a mistake. Even though we wanted the best for him and knew communication was necessary for a fulfilled life, we were also blinded by our own love of words and spoken language. The words I choose even now to describe Charlie, a tendency learned from my parents, I realize, prioritize language above all else. Words have been my longest, most consistent conduit to understanding my brother's life. It would take me years to understand him as someone who did not need them in the same way I did. Remembering how seriously he played, I now believe my brother was a child who had a brain brimming with nonverbal intelligence, his sharp mental energy crackling with intensity.

My Brother's Roller Skates

What did they do in winter, the street slick with run-over ice, the snow pounded like rolled-out dough? What did they do while I was away, Charlie a grinding gear in the tight walls of the house, our mother chasing after him? I can see her sit him down on the kitchen floor and take his left foot with its worn leather shoe into her hand. She would set the sole in place between the metal brackets of the roller skate, and then fix his right foot in the other skate. She tightened the key until both skates were snug. She lifted him up, steadied him, as he glided over the kitchen linoleum and hallway carpet back to his room with its one bed. She kept the door open. There he could do what he'd wanted to do all morning: glide and crash from wall to wall in the tiny room with the spitball–coated ceiling. The bare window he looked through, skating by—white yard, blue sky—glowed in the snow shine of winter. To see and move at the same time was the hinge of his boy's consciousness, how he learned the world. When he spoke the word "tree" we watched him become an acrobat—arms high, palm touching palm, fingers flared, as leaves, as pine needles. More words he shouted when prompted were a visual glimpse, a blink—"sky blue," "cloud white," "tree green" in his inverted grammar. He skated the wooden rink of his mind in that bedroom, the circle he embraced, the spiraling loop of consciousness: his echoes, his terrors and quirks. How can a person know himself, I wonder now, until childhood enters a room where a thousand windows open? Back and forth, he rumbled the small box of a house, blessedly solid, lasting beyond childhood, beyond death. In 1965, when a neighbor at the front door asked what the racket was, my mother said, "He's roller skating in his bedroom."

Blue Stitches in a Pattern

On nights when Charlie was finally settled down in bed, and my father was working late at the newspaper, my mother stayed up waiting for him to come home. Across her lap was a linen tablecloth, seven feet in length, which she was embroidering in cross-stitch that told the story of the classic blue willow pattern. When I imagine her bent over her embroidery, it's winter, all the lights are off in the house except the one near her. She is thoughtful and focused on creating something she knows will come out well. Decades later as I unfold the tablecloth and smooth down the white-as-snow linen, I remember the story depicted in the blue embroidery of two fleeing lovers transformed into doves who meet in the sky above fishermen on a bridge. The story my mother told me was a simpler one about a runaway girl instead of a girl in love. As a child, I stared and stared at the bent willow trees, worked in navy and light blue stitches and wondered what the girl was running away from. I asked my mother this question, but she was not inclined to tell me.

I'm not sure how long it took my mother to finish the tablecloth, but I remember she loved it and I did, too. On holidays, my mother laid it out on our dining room table, the bright linen offsetting the dark and light of the willow pattern. Charlie looked on, fascinated as my mother continued the silent ritual of placing a dinner plate for each of us. One of the constants running through my brother's life from childhood through adulthood was delight in seeing the table laid out in preparation for a family dinner.

My mother the speech correctionist and my father the newspaper reporter covering the post-war European diaspora of urban Detroit were devoted to understanding the world by asking questions, shaping and reshaping the stories they witnessed and telling them not only to each other, but relying on them to understand the wider world. Back before them were farmers, merchants, laborers, and another newspaper reporter, my great-aunt Doll who ran the Warrensburg *Daily Star-Journal* when the men were called into action in the 1940s during the war. With Charlie's entry into the family came late night questions that could not be answered, such as why didn't this child speak, why wasn't he curious, why didn't he seek affection? My father wanted to understand if there was a teleological reason for Charlie's disability and my mother, the pragmatist and teacher, wanted to figure out what had happened to her son and how to repair it. She wanted to teach him how to speak and how to take care of himself. Important to both of them was how Charlie would be educated, and grow to lead a life of dignity. Hanging over them was the inevitable question of whether he would have to spend time in an institution. There were no programs for children like him, no methods, no curriculum. These thoughts must have entered my mother's mind as she stitched her embroidery. For both my parents, and for me, too, our thoughts often turned inward, a dialog held in our mind when the outside world fell into either sleep or silence.

One morning as a child I was awakened by the pussy willow tree scraping my bedroom window. Looking outside, I saw brown branches sheathed by silver glass in the morning light. In Southern Michigan, the entire landscape could turn to ice overnight, large sheets covering roads and grass. Even ordinary Mt. Clemens became magically transformed. I looked out to see both the front and backyard covered in uneven patches of ice, the nap of the grass frozen where the wind had bent it. The back door was hard to budge, requiring much pounding and scraping, finally opening with a long screech to let Sam out. "No school today!" my mother declared as I ran from window to window, viewing the frozen street, perfect for skating like the Dutch kids in my favorite book at the time, *Hans Brinker or The Silver Skates*. My day would be filled ice-skating with my friends down frozen Ferris Street, but Charlie wouldn't experience any of this.

I was lucky to find plenty of books to read in our bookcase by the front door that stretched from floor to ceiling and overflowed with histories, novels, biographies of saints and writers, poetry and art. From the time I had started to read in earnest, I would graze these books, picking one up after the other, reading sporadically or sometimes deeply. Months could go by when I forgot about the bookcase, preferring comic books and magazines. When I did choose a book to read, I remember taking in words primarily for their sounds, as in the stories and poems from the Book House series my mother had enjoyed as a child—Robert Burns, Rudyard Kipling and Christina Rossetti. I read for the cadence of words and sleek turn of narrative. I also read to seek information about what it was like to have a brother or sister with a disability. For a long time, I refused to give into the charms of fantasy fiction written for kids my age like *A Wrinkle in Time, Charlotte's*

Web or *The Lion, the Witch and the Wardrobe.* Like the flying Dutchman of the fairy tale, I searched and searched the skies, looking for a home. Nothing would satisfy my hunger—not fairy tales, not fabulist literature. What I wanted had to be literal as pavement, and close to my life as possible. I did find one book, deep in my parents' bookshelf, a slim *Angel Unaware* by Dale Evans Rogers about the family's daughter with Down Syndrome who died young. Imagining Charlie as an angel unaware living among us gave him a unique status, I thought, someone others could value. My pursuit of this knowledge was solitary, almost secretive, and in a way, like my mother's. I wasn't supposed to tell anyone outside the family that my brother Charlie had a disability, but I did, letting the news slip as I said good-bye at the end of the day to my favorite teacher at St. Thecla's, Mr. Roy. I thought it was an interesting fact he should know.

On other winter days after school, I often went away by myself to skate along a tributary of the Clinton River at the bottom of a small hill by Harrington Road. It was a small slice of land with shallow woods. I am grateful for so much of my childhood, but the one thing, aside from my relationship with Charlie, I revere most is my memory of those woods. As soon as the pale winter sun edged the top of the trees, I was told, I had to come home. Without my friends and my brother Charlie, I had less than an hour to follow the narrow creek beyond the brown bushes, to trace the frozen shape of the ice on my skates. I entered another world known only to me, framed by icy bushes and glass-lit branches, silent except for my brushing skates and the snow-muffled roar of traffic in the distance. In those moments, I could have been the runaway girl in the blue willow pattern, or more like my mother, alone with her thoughts, stitching through the night.

ECHO, ECHOLALIA

If each person has, and I believe we all do, a yearning for beauty that comes from our unique experience of the sensual world, the sense of sound, color and taste fulfilled this desire in Charlie. Music often grounded him and inspired him to dance or sing. Through the experience of color and taste he felt delight in an energy that animated the world around him, inspiring his curiosity. These senses gave him pleasure and calmed him while offering cognitive stimulation, I think. Throughout his life my brother and I made use of this childhood vocabulary rooted in colors, flavors and old songs, a language all its own.

I learned how to communicate with Charlie by first observing him and guessing what he felt, in a kind of trial and error, to get a response. Like any child eager to please I also imitated my mother's attempts to communicate with him. She always told me that as a child, I could understand him even better than she could. Often, I helped her de-code his agitated hand-flapping and squeals when a noise disturbed him, or his shirt was buttoned the wrong way. Sometimes I was right, sometimes not. When he was distressed, language had its limits, and what he really needed was for a discordant noise to end, or a glaring light to be shut off.

In addition to Charlie's sensory vocabulary, the dominant feature of his language, retained his whole life, was echolalia, a kind of repetitive speech a person with autism may use to echo back what he or she has heard a speaker say. The word echolalia can be traced to the melodious Greek word *lalia*, meaning talk. Also embedded in the word is the Greek myth of Echo, the nymph whose voice was punished by the goddess Hera when her chatter distracted the goddess from spying on the erotic antics of her husband, the god Zeus. The nymph's altered voice described by Ovid in *The Metamorphoses*, could be the very definition of echolalia: "of many words her ears have caught, she just/ repeats the final part of what she has heard." What I find most striking is the loneliness of this gentle nymph, eventually rebuffed by the young Narcissus and then shunned by the deities, her body disintegrated. Echo then lived on in the mountains, hills and valleys merely as a voice. The handsome Narcissus was just as haunting a figure, the boy who refused affection and who, in Allen Mandelbaum's translation of Ovid, "had much pride within his tender body: no youth, no girl could ever touch his tender heart." Here Narcissus is almost a portrait of a boy with autism, or a portrait of what many of us non-autistics *assume* a person with the syndrome feels: "If I could just be split from my own body!/ The strangest longing in a lover: I/ want that which I desire to stand apart from my own self." The split did occur—Narcissus's body vanished, his longing for his own watery image in the pool unrequited. All that remained was a yellow and white flower floating in a clear pond. The myth of Echo and Narcissus, an ancient story of autism, or a version of it.

Yet echolalia isn't a negative or even an unusual trait. Echolalia can be a form of language, and a way for child or adult with autism to interact with the world, autism researcher Barry M. Prizant explains. In many children who don't share other autistic traits, echolalia may surface and then disappear as the child achieves better language fluency. In some forms of echolalia whole sentences are repeated; in the form Charlie acquired, echolalic word fragments were recycled and used as a stand-in for making requests, or communicating comprehension. In this unusual language Charlie could, at long last, by the age of six or seven, make himself known to his family. "Charlie want water?" "Charlie want cookie?" "Charlie want go outside?" These words he used were in imitation of questions asked him, a particular form of echolalia sometimes seen in persons with autistic traits. Instead of saying, "Can I have a drink of water?" he would forgo the first person "I" and repeat his name, and then the tag ending of the question. He did this his whole life, persistently resisting the use of "I" even though my family tried many times to help him switch over to the first-person pronoun in his speech. It was an unnecessary worry.

Many theories exist about language acquisition in children. In *The Language Instinct,* Steven Pinker makes the case for a "critical period" in our ability as a species to learn language. Briefly summarized, the idea is that after the age of six or six and a half, a child will not be able to acquire fluent language. The language spoken will be unusual, with mixed syntax, lack of pronouns, and other non-fluent features of language and speech. The strongest illustration of this "critical period" idea is the case of Genie, a child who had endured abuse in the home she lived in for thirteen years. When social workers rescued her, Pinker writes, she could only put together unusual sentences such as these: "Mike paint." "Applesauce buy store." "Genie have Momma have baby grow up."

Pinker contrasts this story of Genie with that of Isabelle, assisted at the age of six and a half when she was found living with a mother with intellectual disabilities. Isabelle was taught fifteen hundred to two thousand words and within a year she was making complex statements such as: "Do you go to Ms. Mason's school at the university?" Pinker's belief is that after the tender age of six and a half, the language learning window closes, for evolutionary and biological reasons, weakening our ability to acquire fluent mastery. Some mastery is possible, but the use of language will never rise above a basic level. Pinker points to studies of deaf children who did not acquire sign language until they were adults; they never do as well as those who learned it beginning in infanthood or early childhood.

Since Pinker's book was published in 1994, neurological studies of brain activity in children have shed more light on the enormous feat by a child in its first year to learn to speak. We are programmed in utero to attend to the sounds of language and voices, a process that gains speed after birth. Up until the end of twelve months, a baby is quickly learning all the phonemes of his native language. Then by a baby's first birthday, he or she has mastered all the sounds of that language. This is why it is so enormously difficult to learn a language in later life and speak it without an accent. Babies are the master linguists. According to Dehaene, in an update of Pinker's theory, this rapid period of learning is called the "sensitive period." He identifies the period as *sensitive* rather than *critical* because within that time, "the capacity [to learn language] shrinks but never truly reaches zero." Also, during that period, a baby is mastering syntax, the movement of words within a language. Without this early development, a child will not be able to understand the positioning of words. This is one reason that children who are born deaf need to have an exposure to a language, including sign language, or a spoken language (with cochlear implants) within the first year of life. A child who learns sign demonstrates features of syntax in language fluently.

I am not sure why my brother experienced deficits in language. He seemed for whatever reason to miss the sensitive deadlines of language mastery, even though he learned some language. Once missing this period of learning, caused by a neurological disorder (most likely autism), Charlie was not able to interact in the social world surrounding him. Instead of moving forward in cognition and intelligence, he declined, or was only able to master simple rote statements and basic self-care such as brushing his teeth, tying his shoes, and getting dressed. Although he never achieved fluency, in the sense you couldn't sit down and have a give-and-take conversation with him, he continued to learn new words for specific, concrete things throughout his life. Dehaene would say he retained plasticity within his brain because for some unknown reason, the capacity for learning vocabulary through adulthood never wanes. There is no sensitivity period for this learning. That ability helped him enormously as he grew into adulthood.

The mystery of Charlie's speech and comprehension, his use of echolalia, his wide vocabulary of colors and foods, his singing and expressions of what he saw in nature, such as rivers, lakes, and trees, never changed. We so wanted him to expand his speech to include initiating conversation, commenting on his feelings, expressing a desire. This never happened. I know I'm not alone in this yearning to connect with an adult family member who is only partially verbal. I've heard how other families with relatives who have autism, aphasia or dementia share a version of this one vivid dream: the loved one is sitting at a table surrounded by family before dinner. Unannounced, this person who hasn't spoken aloud in years or ever before, stands up and turns to everyone in the family, looks each one in the eye and speaks with clarity, tenderness and humor. The relative we love doesn't stop talking, as if they've been away from home for a very long time. I've had this dream over and over. Each time I wake with the realization that no, Charlie has not turned and spoken to me, his sister Cathy, not bared his soul, not confided his feelings of joy or sadness or his memory of a day in our childhood, kept silent for decades.

III
BORN AMONG WOLVES,
HE LEARNED GRACE

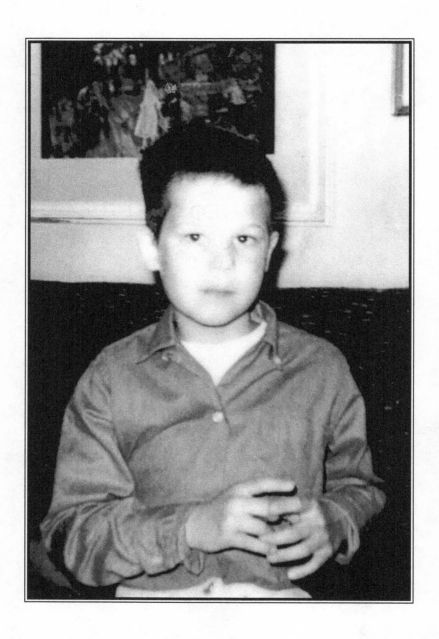

Black and White Squares

I have a snapshot of Charlie at Christmas time sitting on our beat-up couch. His dark, round eyes show the sheen of childhood delight—delight, one would think, with the glitter of a Christmas tree, or the dance of elves in a holiday song. Instead, it was the camera's flash, what we once called a "cube," with its pulse of white light that won his smile. Other photographs of us all together spin like the wheel of life: black and white squares, edges torn with the faint print of a date on the side. The majority are random, unposed shots of small spaces: two children sprawled on worn carpet in a room cluttered with newspapers; our mother in her nightgown feeding our baby brother; a dog licking his paws on a couch covered by a rug; or a child peeking through the torn hole in the living room blinds. These photographs fill silent spaces left empty. It is a way to bring family so distant and lost into the present. The ritual of creating photographs—waiting for the familiar smile, the attention or inattention of the person photographed, and then, the outdated habit of opening an envelope of photos and taking them in your hand—can be a kind of healing. Touching the tangible, paper presence of memory and looking into a still photograph, I see things I wouldn't ordinarily recognize in three-dimensional life, a moment that becomes an emblem because it refuses to disappear. And there's another paradox in the ritual of looking—one that magnifies how we can both have what we've wanted in an image yet know it will never be ours again.

WHERE HAVE YOU BEEN, MY BROTHER?

In a documentary film, a little girl sits in a rocking chair swaying back and forth as she looks out a tall window at the Lapeer State Home, a residential center for people with intellectual disabilities. The film, *A Wind is Rising*, was produced by a Flint television station in 1962. The girl has been given no name. A deep-voiced narrator asks the question, "Where have you been, little girl?" as the camera scans the clouded window and bleak winter outside. The voice, ominous yet steady, continues reciting what seems to be a child's fanciful verse: "I have been riding a pony and picking berries in the woods." As the camera captures the snow-filled institutional grounds, the narrator asks another question, "Where are you going, little girl?" and then provides the answer in that same slow voice: "I am going home."

The Lapeer State Home was about an hour's drive north of Detroit, the closest institution to our home in Mt. Clemens. The girl in the beginning of this documentary lived with thousands of other "souls," many with "mental retardation," the term we heard then, repeatedly, to describe intellectual disabilities. The narrator of the film makes another arresting statement: the little girl in front of the window at Lapeer is a "citizen of a city of 3,600." For her and the thousands like her, the Lapeer State Home is "their woods, their streams, their earth, their whole universe until the day they die."

The sonorous voice and the gray-toned film flecked white chilled me to the bone.

I came upon this archival YouTube documentary of the Lapeer State Home as I was researching the Michigan institutions where Charlie spent eight years of his childhood, beginning in 1965. Most of his eight years were spent at another institution in southwest Michigan, but he did live for almost two years at Lapeer (the name changed during the time to the Oakdale Center for Developmental Disabilities) in the early 1970s before finally coming home to my parents who had by then moved to Kansas City, Missouri. I couldn't find anything about his institution, and became intrigued by the footage of this one. From the distance of time, I can see a resemblance between this little girl in a rocking chair caught by the camera at Lapeer and what my brother looked like as he sat in front of a window, rocking. I watched the documentary over and over. I told my friends about it. I had dreams about it.

What I learned: an additional six hundred citizens of Lapeer State Home were classified as convalescent. The residents were aged eight years old to sixty-two years old. Hundreds of children and adults were gathered together to spend eight hours per day in four "gymnasium-like living rooms," the voice stated, with no educational enrichment, no guidance and under the supervision of few staff. The Home served children and adults from forty-three counties. Throughout the whole institution only one psychiatrist provided care.

In the documentary, the camera switches to a large administration building set back from trees and intersecting sidewalks. You can see in the background a line of tall brick buildings that look to have been built in the Victorian era, or the early 1900s. When the name Lapeer would come up in my family's reluctant discussions of possible places for my brother Charlie's future education and care, those old buildings were what I saw in my mind's eye. The sound of the name "Lapeer" with its echo of the word "peer," indicated to me, a covert, mysterious glimpse of something forbidden. An intrusion, a forbidden peek.

The narrator tells us that although there is "a grimness" on the inside with sterile, sprawling buildings, "there is a warmth within its confines, a care, a devotion." He speaks of the home's impressive energy, what may surprise those who don't know about places like Lapeer, he states, people who remain "smugly safe." The documentary, intended to cast a light on the overcrowded conditions of the Lapeer State Home, won a Peabody Award that year.

I felt sullied watching this, knowing how much my mother and father detested Lapeer.

When the film came out over fifty years ago, I must have seen it on television, thus the appearance of ghosts in my sleep. Certainly, my mother and father saw it. At one time, both of them had visited the institution. I remember a dark buzz in their talk after they returned. My mother definitely didn't want Charlie "sent there" in her words because it was too "institutional" even though it was not as far away as other institutions. He would be locked away in a multi-storied building, she told me. So high up he could never play in the grass. Yes, I agreed. Lapeer was a prison. Or a nightmare.

In the 1960s no one knew much about how to care for and teach people with intellectual disabilities. Dr. A. M. Abuzzo, the superintendent of the

Lapeer State Home, looked authoritative in the large overcoat he wore while being filmed outside on the snow-packed grounds. When he was asked to distinguish the different types of people who are cared for at Lapeer, he said that the community fell into a few groups: children and adults who have mental retardation and those with a combination of mental retardation and emotional disturbance. This latter group particularly troubled him because there were not enough services to assist them. In his account, some children began with a diagnosis of retarded and then gradually became psychotic. Due to lack of resources, he conceded, it was impossible in the Lapeer facility to provide isolation rooms for all of those people who had both retardation and psychosis. Nowhere did the word autism come up, even though Dr. Abuzzo's description of what appeared to be psychosis could very well have been the expression of autistic traits.

At the time the documentary was filmed, autism was primarily known as a psychiatric condition, linked to mental illness. Long-term studies of individual cases by Dr. Leo Kanner, the physician to first identify the phenomenon of autism in children, were beginning to cast light on the condition, but there was still limited understanding of it. Even today, autism is hard to diagnose, and only achieved by close observation of behaviors described in the DSM-5 manual that include, among many things, a lack of language, and an intense inner focus. My brother had those issues, along with very poor speech. If he were a child today, he would fit within the current description of autism in the DSM-5 manual. In the 1960s parlance of Lapeer, however, Charlie would have been one of those children with a dual diagnosis of mental retardation and psychosis or schizophrenia.

"What's madness but nobility of soul/At odds with circumstance? . . ." Saginaw poet Theodore Roethke asks in his poem "In a Dark Time," lines that still resonate with me whenever I think of that era. Roethke died a year after this documentary came out.

〉❋♡❋〈

In March of 1965 when Charlie was eight years old, my parents discovered Fort Custer State Home, further away than Lapeer, about two and a half hours west of us in rural Augusta, but a much better fit for him. Fort Custer, like Lapeer, was one of about half a dozen institutions in Michigan that provided residential care for thousands of children then identified as mentally retarded. Scattered all over the state, these institutions provided varying levels of basic care. In some places, individuals were offered education, such as self-care, minimal reading, writing, basic arithmetic, and crafts, all dependent on the individual's perceived IQ level. At the time of Charlie's institutionalization, according to Michigan's State Mental Health Department, the total population of mentally retarded individuals was 10,538. Of that number, 4,763 were nineteen years old or younger and 5,700 were over the age of twenty-one.

My parents' decision to send my brother to Fort Custer was a sad one, an emotion they hid well in a stoic, stiff-upper-lipped manner they had become used to presenting. This was a decision recommended by physicians for years, and one they had resisted until now. Because I could feel the impending change in the loss of our brother, I was sad, too, and unable to put it into words. When I was eleven, right before Charlie was sent to Fort Custer, we had to take him for a medical exam again at the University of Michigan. It had been a hard day for him. My parents decided to stop for dinner at a well-known restaurant near St. Thecla's, owned by the family of a boy in my class. Charlie was tired and screaming as we sat, ready to order. My friend's father came up to my mother and asked us to leave. We did, immediately, my mother with an enraged look on her face. I was humiliated by Charlie's behavior and my mother's angry response, worried my friend would hear about the incident. My mother was a teacher at St. Thecla's, after all. I never wanted to experience that humiliation again.

In a three-page letter from my father that I've kept, dated in early December of 1991, he has responded to questions I'd asked about what it was like to raise Charlie in the mid-1960s and make decisions about his care. My mother had been forthright with me about her feelings, but my father was always reticent and I knew a letter would be the best way to express his feelings. I thought my questions were gently probing as I realized my parents would be somewhat defensive in explaining their decision to place him in Fort Custer. It had been a major one, requiring them to legally give up their child and designate him a "ward of the state." My father's letter is mostly typewritten, covering both sides of thin, onion-skin paper. He is brief and careful. His disclosures are the most candid he would ever be about my brother. He writes, "You must understand that there were no facilities for the retarded except state institutions or private ones at that time. One doctor told us that all the private places did was to prepare them for the inevitable state hospital." Though doctors recommended Charlie be institutionalized, my parents were not about to forget him, as they were urged to do by some doctors, I remember my mother had told me. Nor would they let him become part of experiments involving an operation on his brain, what one physician suggested when he was young. What that entailed, I never was able to find out.

Because Charlie could not speak, my father writes in his letter, it was also hard to know when something was physically wrong with him. Once, Charlie fell out of bed and my parents noticed the next day that he held his shoulder differently even though he seemed to show no pain. My parents took him to the hospital and found out he had broken his collar bone. That incident came back to me: I remember being alone in the waiting room in the middle of the night while my parents took Charlie into the exam room. Down the hall I saw Charlie whisked away in a wheelchair gliding over the brown linoleum floor by a nursing nun in a long habit. I yelled out to bring him back, and someone may have come to calm me down. Another time, my father wrote, Charlie accidentally hit my mother in the head as he moved a garbage can. My father notes, "And Charles was getting bigger and bigger. Your mother could not handle him during the day and often called me at the office to describe the difficulty she was having." In addition to trying to find a diagnosis for his puzzling condition, they had searched every affordable possibility in an era when public schools were not required to provide even minimal schooling for children like him who were dually diagnosed with both intellectual disabilities and another vague, unspecified term of the times, mental illness. Life in a state home was my parents' last choice for Charlie.

Every family from the 1960s has its cache of family photographs—birthdays, Christmas, First Holy Communion celebrations or weddings. Most are posed with the mother in the center, flanked with gap-toothed kids, all dressed in their very best. My father delighted in aiming his Kodak on us by surprise. The curled, glossy rectangles with dates printed in minute sans serif on the side show the background of an unposed, chaotic, family life: a table of dirty dishes after a Sunday breakfast, my mother and I lounging with the dog on the floor. An ashtray full of cigarette butts rests on a coffee table next to an easy chair swathed in plastic. In one, my brother Charlie appears in cut-off shorts, his moving hands and legs a blur as he speeds through the front yard. In another one, my father is a tall shadow, taller than a tree in the late afternoon light—at once family protector and documentarian with his palm-sized camera.

Another photograph of the last night Charlie spent at home with us in Mt. Clemens marks a turning point in our family. To look at it always makes me sad. The house is neat, with newspapers cleared away and ash trays emptied, as if we were celebrating a holiday. My brother wears a suit and a small Tyrolean hat. I'm wearing my best red dress. Not pictured is my mother's blue-willow-patterned tablecloth laid out and set with plates in each of our places. This scene always delighted him. He knew what to expect: everyone gathered in their best clothes and food on the way. My parents created a special occasion for his last night at home because they didn't want him to forget us.

Even though Fort Custer was far away, my parents were hopeful that Charlie would do well there. Unlike Lapeer, it was set in the countryside, near the woods, which Charlie loved. To help him calm down in the face of imminent change, my mother would often sit him on her lap with her head close to his and tell him the story of what was going to happen next. She discovered that whenever she did this, he accepted the new event with much more confidence and less agitation. Weeks before he left us for Fort Custer, I heard her describe the different bed Charlie would fall sleep in, how he would get up in the morning with other children and eat breakfast all together in a large room. She also told him how Fort Custer would be like the overnight camp he had gone to the previous summer for kids with intellectual disabilities. Before finding Fort Custer, my parents discovered this camp as the only place that openly, even joyously accepted children with disabilities similar to his. At Fort Custer, Charlie would be with kids just like him. He wouldn't be shunned or feared for his screaming outbursts. He would be surrounded by what he loved most—a woods full of trees, grass and flowers, possibly a pond to swim in. It was an idyllic description. I wanted to believe it as much as she did.

My mixed feelings about Charlie living so far from home would only increase. On Christmas Eve that year, my mother and I filled the house with reindeer and snowmen decorations in delighted anticipation for his first visit home. While my father drove out to Augusta to pick him up, we set the table with the good dishes and candles, knowing he would enjoy it. My mother mixed almond paste and confectioner's sugar to make into his favorite marzipan candy fruits. Outside, the evening light gave the new snow a bluish glow. When Charlie came through the back door ahead of my father, he was breathless with excitement, running from room to room shouting, "Red nose, red nose!" from the Christmas carol he loved. We were thrilled to see him, but we worried that he couldn't keep still.

At first, we all thought he was just wound up after coming home. As Christmas Eve wore on and he resisted eating or going to sleep, it occurred to my parents that something was wrong. He was up most of the night, pacing in circles in his old room even though my mother tried all of her strategies to help him calm down. Not until the early hours of Christmas morning did he finally drop off. A call to Fort Custer confirmed the staff had forgotten to give my father the tranquilizing medication Charlie was currently taking. My parents decided to drive him back that Christmas Day to Augusta for the medication they believed was necessary. Mom would stay home with our little brother, and I would go with my father. Charlie would have to remain at Fort Custer and miss Christmas dinner because my father had no more time off from work to drive back and forth. I put on my new print top and slacks and we bundled Charlie into the back of our blue Volkswagen. Without Charlie, there was no point in sitting together at the table set for Christmas dinner that year. Icy flakes fell in sheets as my father drove, and I told myself to get used to these disappointments, accumulating like snow.

I don't recall Charlie ever coming home again for Christmas, but he may have visited for other holidays. Each year as the Christmas season approached, my mother wrapped packages of cookies and other treats to send him and the children living on his ward. I know she missed him, but both my parents believed, as many did at the time, that children needed to develop separately, away from their parents. During his eight years there, he would learn how to get dressed, tie his shoes and brush his teeth. I am sure that except for holiday parties and a few excursions in the wooded countryside, most of his time was spent with dozens of other kids under the constant noise of a suspended television set in a cement-walled recreation room.

Always lingering was the question of how to define Charlie's condition. In my father's letter to me about his memories, he ends with a handwritten note in blue ink at the bottom, quoting Charlie's most recent diagnosis from a Kansas City doctor as "severe mental retardation and not autism." My mother had probably disagreed. She often noted that since childhood Charlie had differed dramatically from his peers with intellectual disabilities because he could not socialize easily or initiate speech, two critical autistic traits. Why was my father so willing to accept this doctor's diagnosis? I think the answer may have been this: the term mental retardation, while carrying a greater stigma (from my family's point of view), had finality and clarity. My father, the stoic journalist, wanted a black-and-white answer, one that could not be softened by calling Charlie's condition autistic. He probably thought that my brother's condition was set in stone and the decision to place Charlie in a state institution years ago unavoidable. I sensed a strong tone of resignation and almost apology in his words. Strangely, in this same letter he writes, "One of the characteristics of his playing was that he would take toys and line them up in perfectly straight rows and become hysterical if anything was done to disturb his display." Elsewhere he recalls that Charlie was beginning to settle into learning from my mother and our babysitter Ollie Nichols, who "did much to add to what your mother had been teaching him—colors, numbers, and how to write his name." This is a description of a little boy with intelligence and autistic traits, but my father could not see it.

ᎧᎧᎧᎧᎧ

What my father didn't include in his letter from 1991 but what I remember, clearly confirmed in another online search, is a *Life Magazine* article with the abhorrent headline "Screams, Slaps, and Love," and the subtitle, "A surprising, shocking treatment helps far-gone mental cripples." It appeared in the spring of 1965, three months after my parents took Charlie to Fort Custer. My mother, father and I all read the long article that detailed the success of experimental operant conditioning methods developed by Ole Ivar Lovaas to treat some of the most difficult behaviors of children with autism: inability to stop hurting themselves, inability to use language, and inability to connect with family. Truly, the details were shocking, documented in bracing photographs of children being yelled at and frightened into halting their antisocial behaviors. The Lovaas method required constant one-on-one work with the child to encourage him to extinguish these damaging behaviors. Punishment was doled out when the child behaved incorrectly; hugs were given when the child reformed. We were at once transfixed by the article's accurate description of behavior similar to Charlie's, and also repulsed by the extreme brutality of the treatment. We were depressed to imagine that this was what it would take to cure my brother. The milder methods resembled what my mother had tried at home with my brother: routines for play and separation in his room when acting up. However, those years when he lived at home with us, my parents had found it almost impossible to sustain vigilance over Charlie during all his waking hours, central to the method required for this approach, now known as Applied Behavior Analysis (ABA), to work.

My mother showed the article to our family physician and asked him if he thought autism might describe Charlie's condition. The doctor confirmed her guess. I know she was wondering if she and my father had made the right decision in placing Charlie in the institution. Of course, neither of my parents knew that Charlie's diagnosis very well could have been *autism* and *intellectual disability.* Autism, hard to diagnose and treat, comes with no easy remedies, and our understanding of it is still evolving. It is now known that an estimated thirty percent of people with intellectual disabilities have autistic traits. Whatever the diagnosis, my parents were still left with the dilemma of finding appropriate education and care for him. Like many parents at the time, they were flying blind.

From my parents' point of view, the only community who accepted my brother with open arms was made up of people with intellectual disabilities and their caretakers, who had what they sensed as that same "warmth. . .a care and devotion," described in the documentary. My mother told me she thought Charlie learned as much from the staff in the kitchen at Fort Custer as he did anywhere else. During the years of the early and mid-1960s, an acceptance of mental retardation was gaining a foothold due to the activism of many parents. There were public service announcements referring to it frequently on television, and the Kennedy family made significant funding available. Dale Evans publicly promoted the Association of Retarded Citizens, the primary nonprofit organization founded by parents on behalf of their children. In the midst of this new awareness, compassionate on the surface, there was a strange underside: the normalization of institutionalization.

My parents still felt significant shame in having to place my brother at Fort Custer and were reluctant to share their distress with their own families or our neighbors. I was told never to mention that Charlie now lived there. Collected in a box are all of my father's news clips from the time he worked as a reporter covering the immigrant communities of Detroit. In one clip dated December 15, 1965, nine months after Charlie was taken to Fort Custer, the headline reads: "News Reporter Honored for Nationality Coverage." I remember this occasion, what my mother called my father's testimonial dinner, a gathering organized by representatives of the Polish, Hungarian, Serbian, Latvian, Ukrainian, Italian and Asian communities to thank my father for his reporting on events of importance to them. It was the custom at such dinners to collect money the honoree would then donate to a favorite charity. In his testimony, the Right Reverend Monsignor Vincent Borkowicz of St. Stanislaus Church stated that my father "has covered all groups in our city with compassion, understanding, and objectivity." My father's cousin, Father James Enright, a hockey coach at Catholic Central High School, gave the invocation but he was the only family member other than my mother to attend. A picture of my mother beside my father shows her as strikingly beautiful, dressed in a black cocktail dress with lace edging the neck and sleeves. Her jet-black hair and olive skin are offset by the red lipstick she wore as her only touch of makeup. Her head is upturned as she listens to my father accept his honor. Embedded in the article is this sentence: "Proceeds from the dinner are earmarked for retarded children at Fort Custer State Home and Training School." The story does not state why that particular institution was chosen. The article is unsigned but I know my father wrote it.

The year Charlie had to leave us, our house, once filled with noise, became much quieter even though my little brother, at the age of two, babbled in the background. Charlie's bedroom was cleaned up now: my mother had scraped off the dried-up spit balls Charlie had flung to the ceiling of his bedroom where they hung like paper stalactites. My friends who had stayed away from our house because they were afraid of Charlie's erratic behavior and his high-pitched squeals out of the blue could now come over to play with me or my brother Bill. We began to settle into middle-class stability, but the certainty that all of us—my mother, my father, and myself—had failed tremendously by sending Charlie away and not making a home for him penetrated my thoughts. I now had a normal life, but at what cost?

Our visits to Fort Custer were few and far between. Our family only had one car and my father had little time off. As we drove to visit Charlie, I watched the flat industrial landscape of metropolitan Detroit become a countryside of sugar beets, oats and beans, apple and cherry fields. Exotic to me were the brick barn silos with spare two-story white clapboard houses surrounded by shelter trees and beside them, glass-covered cold frames for growing mangelwurzel and turnips. On the flat highway, mirages often appeared in the distance, huge puddles of water that vanished once you approached. Further west, the table-top terrain would become a roller-coaster ride for a few miles as my mother announced, "We're in the Irish Hills!" The excitement was short-lived before the land turned flat and familiar again.

Closer to Fort Custer, the road was rough asphalt with chickweed peeking up between the cracks. In the distance grew low trees—willows, maple saplings—and beyond were blocks of army barracks edged by weeds, the mustard yellow exterior of the barracks peeled and cracked. An army training center and prison to hold captured German soldiers, Fort Custer was repurposed sometime in the 1950s as a state home for children with intellectual disabilities. A veteran's cemetery and a small body of water, a creek or river, lay in the background. This was where Charlie lived those eight years of his childhood. The first time I saw it, I could see why my mother said it was like a camp and I tried to imagine the best for him: hikes in the woods, songs, and swimming. A canteen sold candy bars and soda pop, and on our visits, we could hang out there at picnic tables or walk around where metal chairs lined the area. Inside the administrative office, the floors were brown linoleum, and the furniture was built to last in the early mission style of heavy, dark oak.

On our visits, Charlie beamed when he saw us, and he continued to smile throughout the time we spent with him. I noticed right away that his thick brown hair was shaved, like all the other boys, to prevent lice. We always went out for lunch at Howard Johnson's in Battle Creek where we ate hamburgers and had mint chocolate chip ice cream. When we returned to Fort Custer, Charlie would run as fast as he could away from us to the front door of his barracks. We never took it personally. We understood that he was going back to the safety of what he knew now as his home with the metal bed he shared in a room of other boys and their metal beds.

On one trip, I remember a little boy a few years younger than me who asked if he could show me a chair he'd made. He returned with a misshapen collection of boards nailed together in all directions, proudly thrusting it toward me for inspection. I didn't know quite what to say, but I cheered him on, telling him he'd done a good job. He quickly ran off. Later, during that same visit, I was introduced to the ward where the girls lived. In contrast to the boys, these girls didn't yell or run across the floor. A few stood and stared at me for a long time. Who wouldn't stare at a strange girl standing by their beds?

I felt mystified seeing all those kids at Fort Custer and thought about them long after our trip home. These were children who shared my generation, existed in the same world, at the same point in time, yet my life was so different from theirs. I could read and write, go to school, enjoy my friends. I lived in a house and had my own bedroom. As a teenager, I could sense more freedom coming my way, the future unrolled before me. That day I tried not to feel superior to the children I met, or display the confusion I felt. Mainly, I didn't want anyone, including my parents, to sense my anxiety.

Awareness of the inferior care for people with intellectual disabilities who lived in institutions happened gradually. During World War II, conscientious objectors served as aides in many institutions, and probably felt the same sense of moral anxiety as I did when visiting my brother. Some documented what they saw through photographs, essays and diary entries. Authors John Donvan and Caren Zucker report in their book on autism, *In a Different Key*, how journalists on reading these testimonies became interested in the unregulated conditions of institutions for people with intellectual disabilities. In one example, the *Charleston Gazette* published an article by Charles Armentrout in 1949 about the Huntington State Hospital, exposing the dangerous conditions there, including fire traps, signaling a clarion call to do something. In 1952, a lethal fire swept through the building and within minutes took the lives of fourteen residents, all female.

No doubt the majority of those children at Fort Custer, like the kids at the Lapeer State Home, had undiagnosed autism as well as intellectual disabilities. The nobility of their souls was certainly at odds with the circumstance of their lives. I never heard about isolation rooms at Fort Custer, but they could have existed. More stories of neglect at the Lapeer State Home documented in the film, *A Wind is Rising*, have appeared in books and various news articles. Of the old mustard-colored wooden buildings of Fort Custer State Home, however, few recorded accounts exist. In 1971, five months after our last visit to see Charlie when he was fourteen and a half, the state closed it down, citing budgetary issues in a letter to my parents. A rare newspaper article of the time period reported that state officials made the decision to close when Fort Custer's wooden buildings were judged to score a "three-minute burn rate," meaning all the buildings could go down in flames within that short amount of time. My brother was known as a fast runner and he always displayed a cautionary, almost phobic approach to burning candles. How did he become so careful? Was he taught to run for safety after witnessing a fire at Fort Custer he couldn't comprehend? We'll never know.

My brother didn't have the words to describe his years at Fort Custer State Home, but once, I believe, he came close. On our last trip there to visit him, Charlie had grown tall and lanky, wearing a red-and-white windowpane check shirt with his name inked on the collar in my mother's black penmanship. In a photograph from that day, his tanned arms wing out of this shirt with his head tilted back as he chugs a bottle of Canada Dry in the Fort Custer canteen. I remember talking with him in our usual mode to encourage speech—asking him what he liked to eat, pointing out colors and cars. He then turned to me and uttered a stream of words that sounded like a story or an opinion, but I couldn't understand him. My brother wasn't speaking in a dream, but it felt like it. For the first time, he was initiating a conversation, perhaps a request for more soda pop, or he could have been telling me where he'd been all those years, far from home. He was looking intently at my face, my mouth. I wished I could have understood him as I listened, nodding my head, telling him to keep talking.

Black Dog

After Charlie's departure the rhythms of our house changed forever. I remember noting unusual pockets of time when there was not one noise in the house except my little brother's chatter as he floated through imaginary worlds of play, something Charlie never did. My friends could now come over to visit and we played giggling games without disruption. Yet, our house seemed to have been marked for tragic loss. One of the kids in the neighborhood asked me, "What happened to your brother?" I didn't know how to answer him. Told by my parents to say nothing, nothing was what I felt, a hollowness. Charlie's bureau was empty of clothes. His shoes were gone. My brother Bill moved from a bed in my room to Charlie's old bedroom. His main possessions—his bed, marbles, and roller skates—were passed on to Bill. The house resonated with voices, but the tone was off.

In sixth grade, within that first year after Charlie left, I saw a purple and orange lightning-shaped streak pulse in front of my eyes as I took a math test. Later, I came down with a severe headache followed by nausea. My teacher assumed I was trying to get out of taking the test and reluctantly let me go home. This headache, which returned every few months, cast my mother into a new cascade of worry as she sat by my bed while the nausea subsided. I was the second child of hers to exhibit a strange, neurological ailment. I felt as if I had let her down by harboring this unusual illness. Outwardly she projected calm, but I didn't trust her to remain at ease for very long. By the time I was thirteen it was clear I needed to get an electroencephalogram (EEG), the main tool for testing brain abnormalities at the time.

At the EEG appointment, a nurse stuck over a dozen pins of electrodes into my scalp, small pricks that nicked the skin. I was told to lie back on a paper-covered table and count to ten. I couldn't fall asleep in the middle of the afternoon, and so I was told to begin reciting familiar names— "Mom, Dad, Billy, Charlie, Sam, George (our guinea pig), Ferris Street, Harrington Road." As I drifted off into the first phase of sleep, a purring machine turned out pages inked by a stylus that followed the rhythms of my brain. I wasn't sure how long I slept. It was a strange feeling to wake, at the age of thirteen, and look over to the machine with its pages and pages of my printed brain waves, this record of my consciousness, what I had tried, along with my newly unfolding body—the curves of my breasts, my hidden hairs—to keep private.

We found out soon that my EEG result was fine, with a slight abnormality, in contrast to Charlie's EEG, my parents told me, which was completely normal. I remember how, after we received the all-clear news from the doctor who explained my headaches as migraine, which could be managed, my father yanked a few frayed strands from the worn-out turquoise carpeting, then pulled up a whole swath, almost in celebration. Delighted, he moved through the living room, tearing up carpet as he went. He pushed furniture out of the way, pulling back the throw rugs they'd placed over the thread-bare holes. He told me to boil water on the stove, and when it was ready, he poured it over more carpeting, exposing the hardened glue underneath. He took off and brought back a filled gasoline can, told us to get out of the area as he carefully poured a little over the patches, waited for the gasoline to soak in, and then ripped up the rest in wide, heavy swatches. I then had to pour more water on the area to dilute it. I wouldn't recommend this. The smell of gasoline, rubber and wood was overpowering. A few days later my father rented a sander and blasted it over the bumpy glue-roughened floors in the living room and hallway. My mother pitched in as they both laughed and worked with amateur speed, seeming to enjoy every moment. My little brother and I helped by hoisting discarded carpeting out to the garage. Once the sanding was completed, my father applied brown stain in fast Jackson Pollock swirls over the roughly sanded floors, leaving wide circles of uneven marks, resembling, I think now, what the inside of his mind must have been at the time. Relief seemed to fill the house—the carpeting was out and I was healthy.

Yet it must have been a guilty feeling, this relief. Charlie was the central mystery of our family, his life shaping how we looked at the world. In my father's letter from the 1990s, I'd finally learned what he thought about being a father to Charlie. His letter gave me a glimpse into those rough, uncertain years. At the time my father wrote, Charlie was launched as a young adult working in a sheltered workshop, living in a group home. The turbulent days of Charlie's childhood on Ferris Street and his years at Fort Custer were in the past. In that letter, my father could now offer a perspective in writing, from a distance, as he was used to doing. But it was my mother's frank, immediate account of motherhood narrated in the kitchen that has stayed with me.

What I heard many times from my mother: her cautionary tale never to have children. She was not subtle about that advice. Her motivation was to protect me from experiencing the pain of having a child who suffered a severe, puzzling illness. This was an aspect of motherhood she found most difficult. Forthright and blunt-spoken, she'd wave a strand of wiry hair out of her eyes while she was making dinner, look me straight in the face and declare that motherhood was strenuous, constant, and heartbreaking. I didn't have the personality for it, she would assert, more than once, but in telling me, I knew, she was also recognizing that same difficulty within herself. Poet Adrienne Rich's first recorded journal entry in her *Of Woman Born: Motherhood as Experience and Institution,* could well have been my mother's words: "My children cause me the most exquisite suffering of ambivalence: the murderous alternation between bitter resentment and raw-edge nerves, and blissful gratification and tenderness." Rich describes feeling "weak sometimes from held-in rage." As a young child, I would sometimes come home from school and find my mother curled on the couch, totally worn out. This was her motherhood of worry and work, continually, with no breaks, no let up, no gradual change as her child developed through childhood into adulthood. She was right. I didn't think I could live up to the task if I were handed a similar fate as my mother. I wouldn't marry until late in life and I never had children of my own.

In one of our talks, I remember my mother telling me how sad she felt when she realized I was so frightened of her as a child. Perhaps all children fear their mother's reprimands. My mother was frightening because when she took on what the French call the *black dog* of despair, her outbursts of anger paralyzed me. I was the easiest target: healthy, closeby and unlikely to fight back. My mother probably had a mood disorder, swinging from delightful humor to toxic anxiety. Some moods were glorious, full of delight over a simple project like painting a bedroom, or watching a late-night Alfred Hitchcock movie. Her perspective on current events and human nature was often brilliant, quick, heartfelt. She could capture a neighbor's or a relative's voice hours later, in a way that could make my father laugh so hard, I'd hear him from the basement where I rode my bike.

My mother was also able to project a depth of understanding in the midst of confusing events. Even as a child I could sense this. After the death of John F. Kennedy, the country came to a standstill. On the day of his assassination, many of us were let out early from school to find our parents in tears in front of the television. That's where I found my mother, who had arrived home from St. Thecla's before I did. It was only the second time I had ever seen her give in to tears. At the Democratic convention occurring many months later, Bobby Kennedy quoted from Shakespeare's *Romeo and Juliet* in a commemorative speech for his brother. After the speech was over, my mother walked through the house, reciting those beautiful lines:

> *Take him and cut him out in little stars,*
> *And he will make the face of heaven so fine*
> *That all the world will be in love with night*
> *And pay no worship to the garish sun.*

   The Kennedy assassination was symbolic for many Americans as a loss of innocence, and end to idealism. For my mother, this feeling was one she may have felt not only over the loss of a president, but for her own diminished dreams for my brother Charlie. Because she felt it, I did, too.

   My mother had very little confidence that any other parent in our neighborhood would understand what she faced with Charlie. Our neighbors on Ferris Street were often bewildered when they witnessed, from afar, his temper tantrums and erratic behavior. I would like to think no one meant to be judgmental and most of them were kind, curious and rightly perplexed, as were we. Our immediate next-door neighbor to the south, however, was negative to the point of hostility, spreading rumors that Charlie had broken into her home, and then urinated in the family's dresser drawers. We often heard similar stories about Charlie as they circulated through the neighborhood, but my mother and father tried to turn it all into comical routines they liked to share with each other. This was the same neighbor who put a sign in her yard, "Keep Off the Grass," about which my mother and father joked that it was aimed at dogs in the neighborhood who could read. When this neighbor accused my family of having too many garbage cans, my father painted the two larger cans "His" and "Hers" and the smaller one, "Theirs."

   Decades later, one day in June I visited our old house in Mt. Clemens. The neighbor next door who had spread all those rumors was still living, well into her nineties. The current owners of our old house who had bought it almost fifty years ago, generously invited me and my friend Robert in to look around. While we were standing in the old kitchen, since expanded beautifully, the owner told me they had learned from the neighbor next door

that a "little boy had lived here who had been locked up by his family."
I gently corrected that version of the story on the spot, telling them that
Charlie had grown up to be a productive, happy person, although his autism
and disability limited his experience. Our hosts immediately understood and
wished my brother well. In that moment, in that house, although I never
showed it, on hearing what our neighbor had said, I felt the sting of cruelty
my mother must have experienced fifty years ago. When we were outside, I
looked at the brown brick house with its upright gable and the overgrown
lilac bush at the side I'd always remembered. The air had turned electric, all
the colors of spring strikingly vivid. My mother was long gone, but if I could
I would have told her that now, finally, I understood her rage, her pain, and
the tears she never could admit.

We Were Taught to Mourn, 1968

The priest at the end of the aisle raised his linen arms to reveal the consecrated host. I heard three bells and the click of rosary beads against pine pews. Six years after Vatican II, the priest faced us, the parishioners, as he conducted Mass at St. Thecla's. I heard a muffled brush of shoes, a cough. We all paused—believers, unbelievers, pilgrims, and doubters. I watched my father half kneel, half sit. Old words from the original Latin Mass fluttered from him as he prayed in the wrong language. I hoped no one else heard. Rain rolled down a high, blue window. Who are we to God in our clamor, our stillness? Who are we to each other? Rain, wood, Latin and smoke.

That morning I could feel the small hairs on the back of my neck stand up like insect legs. The feeling was unsettling, out of my control. I was not sure of its origin. I entered the sleeve of stopped time, and found myself lifted out of the present into another state. I watched the candles, the shuffling parishioners, the swaying priest at the head of the aisle, as if I were not there at all, but at a distance, observing: the Mass at its most sacred moment of two-thousand-year-old time, the miracle when bread is raised over our heads, then broken with the fingers into the palms of the hands. Once broken, the bread becomes body. A tender, living body, held up for us to see. When it was time to take Communion, I remained in the pew, practicing a liquid mental flow in and out that came easily whenever I felt completely calm. Years later I would learn that this flow is both a psychological state, a subconscious move to protect the psyche from trauma, and also a physical one, the brain wooed to a slow beta pulse by droning musical tones or human voices, as in meditation, the chant of prayer, or the recitation of poetry.

I think it may also be the crystal point of doubt from which insight begins to open. Sitting in that pew, I realized I never wanted to enter a Catholic church again. I no longer believed in one, apostolic church. And because in Catholicism, you must enter grace with a pure, determined heart, I decided not to pretend. I was no longer a believer because my questions about birth, sex and death had never been answered in my later years as a Catholic school girl. My peers and I were always on the brink of bursting as we clamored the sister teaching us religion with concerns of who did what to whom: "And who was Saint Joseph? Was he the one who made Mary pregnant?" Before the teacher, our faces floated fiery red, I'm sure, in the echo of our sharp, doubting barbs as we awaited her response. To this sister we were an unruly mob. We were becoming heathens, hippies, draft dodgers. We were that era's fury unloosed—drugs, the Beatles, Mick Jagger, the atom bomb. Our questions were questions that brought down the Kennedy family, led the birth control pill from the laboratory into the corner drugstore. What audacity we showed. Shock and impatience were the answers we got. Years later, it has occurred to me how remarkable it was that all of us in class felt confident enough to even risk asking such sensitive questions about birth and sex. The Felician sisters were strict, but they didn't punish us for pressing them. They just ignored us.

Yet the Church was not comforting; it could be prickly, like the unraveled carpet of our house. Church was not a place to go for answers, for connection, belief, or verified truth. I was at the beginning of a crisis that would last for years—the persistence of doubt, cultural, familial and personal. Of this awareness, Gerard Manley Hopkins, one of the strongest poets of faith and doubt in English writes: "I wake and feel the fall of dark, not day. /What hours, O what black hours we have spent." That day in church, I felt my own hour of unease made more dramatic in the company of believers, similar to the feeling Hopkins describes in another sonnet: "To seem a stranger lies my lot, my life/Among strangers."

That time in my life I believed God had set the world in reverse: beautiful German shepherd dogs turning on civil rights protesters, a handsome young president assassinated in a motorcade; boys out of twelfth grade coming home from war in body bags. And my brother Charlie, born with what everyone called mental retardation, a condition that disqualified him from receiving schooling, health insurance, the love of friends or community, the kingdom granted everyone else. I kept these doubts to myself that Sunday, not wanting to disrupt my father's faith in prayer. I wondered if my mother, at home and not in church, also had her doubts. She did, I would learn later.

I was thirteen going on fourteen. Enormous changes had occurred not only in my family with the departure of my brother Charlie, but within the country as a whole. The Detroit uprising in July the summer before cut short the last time I spent with my grandmother in Saginaw. In the morning after the beginning of the conflict, my grandmother and I looked out the front door facing South Jefferson and noticed cars and trucks speeding at a fast clip. Just as a pickup truck full of white guys pointing their rifles drove by, my grandmother stepped out on the porch. I urged her to get inside. Brian, my friend from the court, came running up our sidewalk to let us know that more men like those in the truck were shooting their rifles off in the air and headed downtown for a confrontation. All across the state, white supremacists were reacting, inspired to take arms and incite trouble. Later that day my grandmother and I were surprised to see my father had come to take me home early, announcing we had to get back before a metro-wide curfew that evening. My grandmother set up a card table in the living room for an early dinner because my father could not fit in the tight kitchen under the eave. On our way home, my father and I watched the National Guard tanks and jeeps maneuver down the highway, headed to Detroit.

The event touched every facet of the city, including our small blue-collar Mt. Clemens. For months there were commentaries on the radio and television about disastrous policies in the city of Detroit that made life for Black Americans a daily struggle. Through our church I learned about the open housing movement to counteract decades of red-lining policies in housing, including our subdivision. I began to look around my completely white neighborhood and wondered, naively, if Black people might now feel safe to move here. As the city of Detroit and the whole country were experiencing a reflection on our involvement in the Vietnam War, and our neglect of civil rights for Black Americans, I began to question not only the religious doctrines I had been taught, but also the civic lessons of patriotism we all had inhaled. The forces that kept down Black communities and justified our involvement in an illegal war were the same forces that required my brother to live in an institution, I concluded, but kept that thought to myself.

A month after the Detroit uprising, my parents told me they could no longer afford St. Thecla's Catholic School. I would start eighth grade in public school. I was elated and threw my cranberry plaid uniform in the trash. My mother had already stopped teaching there after three years. At Clinton Valley Junior High I was told I could choose shop class or aeronautics, while the boys could also choose home economics, if they wanted. As a lover of Amelia Earhart, I was overjoyed to be studying the theory of flight. I still had to sit through catechism classes at St. Thecla's on Tuesday nights, still badgering the teacher who led us through the contradictions of Catholic theology. In early fall my mother told me I didn't have to go to catechism classes anymore because she'd heard from someone at our church that all the kids in the class had been directed to pray for my questioning soul.

Inside me was a series of burning questions I could not articulate: why did Charlie have to live in an institution so far away from us, and why, much to my shame, did his placement bring a sense of relief to me and my family? Could we have done it differently?

I met a girl in our eighth-grade class who inspired the same twinned feelings of annoyance and protection my brother Charlie so often triggered. I knew she was poor because the bus dropped both her and her brother off at a run-down house far in the country. She was overweight with bad skin, a perennial F student who spoke in halting, half-formed sentences. Even though I should have known better, I reacted inconsistently to her overtures toward friendship, welcoming one minute, then shunning her later in small, hurtful ways. I could have invited her to sit at lunch with my friends, but I didn't. I could have returned her phone calls, but I didn't. Because no one suggested that I offer more than the slightest kindness to this lonely girl, I kept her at a distance. She was too frightening to me. She was the specter of what my future would be: an uneven relationship between me and a brother who couldn't speak, couldn't read and write, a boy who would grow up powerless to protect himself.

I picked up my search again for a book about a child like my brother. I found nothing at the library, and at first nothing in my parent's bookcase beyond *Angel Unaware*, which I'd outgrown. Often, when choosing a book from our bookcase, I would first finger the spines, touching the upright shapes in their places on the shelf. If I were by myself on a particular quest for carnal knowledge, I might be lucky enough to land on *The Naked and the Dead*, eager to learn something about being naked (I couldn't imagine being dead). Or I'd delight in Colette's risqué collection of short stories. For a real scare, I'd pick up the biography of Saint Catherine of Sienna, my namesake, with a coiled dog-like Satan vanquished by the saint's foot on the cover. My method was to pick one of these books when no one was watching and read random pages, acquiring what knowledge I could, skimming the pages for hot words like "skin," "breast," "kiss," "mortification."

I may have skipped over this book, or perhaps it came into my view the moment I was ready: *Things As They Are*, by Paul Horgan. The book had a sepia-toned cover that showed a tow-headed boy with an apple in his hand, looking out a lace-curtained window. The picture touched a core of sadness I felt as Charlie's sister. I needed to read it.

Things As They Are is a story about a young boy's coming of age and his reckoning with the fragile integrity of his elders. Horgan's opening words to the most moving chapter of the book refer to the complexities of loving a child with intellectual disabilities in a world that rejects such imperfection, supposedly in kindness: "How do we manage to love at all when there is so much hate masquerading in love's name?" This question announced the disparity more directly than anything I had read at the time. The young narrator, Richard, a friend to John, the child with disabilities, slowly begins to understand the impact of that question in watching the behavior of his peers, and then his elders. Richard's friend is hosed by a group of mocking boys who shout, "John, John, the dog-faced one," while Richard watches it all, helplessly. John's parents don't make a strong effort to call for a doctor when the boy catches pneumonia. They wait out his fever, letting him languish until he dies. After reading this book, I thought not only of how easy it was to overlook Charlie, but also the unnamed young man in Saginaw who lived near my grandmother and the girl at school I often avoided. They were people our culture decided didn't belong. Remembering them made me feel as sad as when I thought of my brother.

Midway in my eighth-grade year, our English teacher, Mr. Phillips, suspended the curriculum and required all of us to study the major issues that had skyrocketed to importance. We spent two days watching the film *Raisin in the Sun* and discussing the Civil Rights Act of 1964 and 1968. After constructing a small aircraft replica in our aeronautics class out of cloth and wood with Mr. Kelley, we studied the Vietnam War, memorizing a map of Southeast Asia. We learned about the Algonquian-speaking peoples who first populated our region banking the Clinton River and whose tribes our schools were named after. In April of 1968, Martin Luther King Jr. was assassinated and in June, right before school closed, we lost Robert Kennedy. Our teachers taught us thoroughly and faithfully. In those spring days sliding into summer, they also taught us how to mourn, an even greater lesson.

GRASS COVERS ALL

On a shelf in my home is a small painting of dark pine trees and umber-tinted hills in Czechoslovakia that had belonged to my father. The scene is painted in oil and on the back are notations of its previous life as a Czech postcard. In the summer of 1968, my father traveled to West Germany with the purpose of entering Czechoslovakia to report on the invasion of Soviet (and Warsaw Pact) troops into the city of Prague. It took him five tries, but he finally made it through, disguised as a worker who prints newspapers rather than a reporter who writes for them. He was one of the few journalists able to report from inside the country. He was gone for several weeks, and although he connected with my mother via telegrams and a rushed phone call, I never had a chance to speak with him. Almost every day, though, I could imagine his voice as I read his stories about the ordinary citizens he interviewed on the streets of Prague, such as the ones who marked up the pavement with signs pointed the wrong way to confuse Soviet tanks. The small painting was a gift from a Czech artist who lived outside the city and remembered my father among the U.S. soldiers who came in to protect the region toward the end of World War II. When I asked Dad how he was able to get so much information from people when he didn't speak the language, he said he always carried a small dictionary, and found students studying English willing to interpret. When I asked him what I needed to do to become writer like him, he had one sober answer: learn to type. And I started that year, typing school assignments and the many plays I dreamed up on our portable Royal.

Later, in early spring of 1969, my father left the paper to become the editor of *VFW Magazine,* located in Kansas City, Missouri, where the Veterans of Foreign Wars (VFW), a nonprofit organization that published the magazine, was headquartered. That March we pulled out of our driveway on Ferris Street for the last time. Our blue Volkswagen was packed with my mother and father, my brother Bill and me and Sam, our Airedale, tucked in the compartment behind the back seat. The move felt nomadic and hasty, as if my parents were escaping an event they couldn't speak about. In some sense, that may have been the case. My father became well known through his almost daily reporting on Czechoslovakia, yet the newspaper insisted he work midnights, the shift he despised after fifteen years. When an opportunity to work in Kansas City, only an hour from his favorite Aunt Doll in Warrensburg, came up, he jumped at the chance. I asked how we would arrange for Charlie to come to Kansas City, but my parents didn't give a clear answer. This bothered me. And I knew I'd also miss my grandmother, left in Saginaw.

Within a few months of moving, my mother's moods became volatile again, like they were when I was a young child. I knew she was thinking about Charlie. My mother had stopped hitting me since I had become a teenager, but had increased her sarcasm when it suited her and she could still be spontaneously punitive. I was very wary of her, keeping my thoughts and questions to myself. Once I rolled my eyes at dinner and she doused my head with a cup of lukewarm coffee. The only heat I felt was humiliation intensified by the combined smell of sugar, milk and coffee in my hair. I had no shampoo in the house and I remember riding my bicycle up 63rd Street to buy a green bottle of Prell at the local Katz drugstore. My mother's impulse was the cap on a rage that had been brewing for months. I thought I should have seen it coming. On another morning only weeks before, I had come downstairs to see dishes broken and cookbooks upturned that she had thrown across the room. She and my father must have had a fight, and I must have slept through it.

Kansas City in the early 1970s seemed deeply conservative. Remnants of segregation could still be seen in the places people lived and shopped. Our neighborhood was built on a former Civil War battlefield. Much to my shock, my parents, who had supported civil rights, and were part of many discussions in Detroit in the aftermath of the uprising in 1967, were making friends with people who proudly admitted their ancestors were part of the Confederacy! Those friendships were short-lived, and my parents, avid history buffs, were perhaps too eager to make new friends. Years later I learned that the original real estate developer of our extensive neighborhood, J.C. Nichols, had established a covenant restricting sales of homes to whites only. My parents had fallen into the same line of thinking of many white liberals: lending support for racial equity at the beginning, but when the issues became more complex or closer to home, quickly removing themselves from engagement and ignoring sharp realities. We were now not living in the South, but clearly on its border. In the small Missouri town of Arrow Rock, not far from Kansas City, I remember seeing a rectangular stone in the middle of town on which enslaved Africans had to stand when they were auctioned for sale. I stared and stared at the indentation in the center smoothed by the feet of hundreds of people. When I asked my parents about this history, they were not inclined to talk.

At Southwest High School where I now attended, there was a reluctance to engage in discussions of a political nature, a deep contrast to my previous school in Michigan. In English class other students shushed me when I made a comparison of Carl Sandburg's line, "I am grass. I cover all" to our collective indifference to the Vietnam War. In another class, a teacher preferred to call the Civil War "The War Between the States." Our football team at Southwest High School was named the "Indians" with no reference to the indigenous Kaw, Osage, or Kickapoo peoples who had once lived in our area of the Midwest and had been removed. In Mt. Clemens, we had been taught the indigenous history of the region since grade school. At Southwest, a girl in my English class who wore a black armband in solidarity with the Moratorium to End the Vietnam War was ostracized. I wanted to join her, and in my old role as a firebrand would have, but in Kansas City, I sensed a reserved attitude in my parents, a desire to fit in and not rock the boat. I held back, and in doing so, entered the paradox of my identify at the time. I was a sister without my closest brother. I was a granddaughter who never saw her grandmother anymore. I was brought up Catholic, but no longer identified with the religion. I was born in the north, and now I lived in a place bordering the south. I was someone who questioned authority and now I was quiet.

Even though I no longer considered myself a practicing Catholic, the internal reasoning of the religion and its rhythms must have still moved me. In Catholic school we had learned about service to others, beyond acquisition and building wealth, often condescendingly described as "helping the poor." That idea most likely seeded my query about economic and social inequality. I was aware of many contradictory worlds, one with my family in a lovely house in a good neighborhood and another, what I saw of Charlie's life in a stark institution. At the same time, I sensed a world of poverty not far away from where we lived. I remember searching for the works of Karl Marx at our high school library and discovered I needed special permission from the librarian to check out *Das Kapital*, which made it even more appealing. Of course, I found the book impossible to read. What I really needed was a wise teacher who could lead me through these large questions. That was another paradox: I wanted to overthrow the old structures, but I also wanted to understand what held the world together if it wasn't God.

I was fortunate that a different kind of teacher walked into my life. Mr. Stark, our eleventh-grade biology teacher, began the first day of class by holding an instrument up in the air in front of us, and then stating its incorrect name. Next, he would put the instrument down and then with emphasis, pick it up again, now stating the correct name. We were instructed to repeat that name and warned never to call a pipette an eyedropper, or a petri dish a saucer. His lessons were dramatic and corny. His style—lab coat, wire-rimmed eyeglasses, serious demeanor—was witless, a kind of character he assumed when he entered the classroom. "Groovy" was his way of giving occasional praise and once we got over the shock of hearing him say it, we realized he was hamming it up for our benefit.

Mr. Stark said we would never remember what we learned. We would forget the genus and phyla of the beloved snake curled in the aquarium at the back of the room. We wouldn't remember the parts of a flower, or how a bee danced its message of honey and light to other bees. We would learn, he stated, how to study. We received that news without argument. In other classes, we ignored our teachers or badgered them, a delaying tactic. For Stark, we were an audience. And he played to us. Every morning was recitation as he stood before us seated alphabetically by last name in rows of black-topped lab tables. He addressed each one of us formally as Miss or Mister, and then asked rote, fact-based questions. We paid strict attention as he went down the rows. When it was our turn, we answered by searching through the notes we were required to take for homework each night.

Mr. Stark was right—it was impossible to remember everything I'd read the night before. I was falling in love with Richard. He was a year older than me, and lived about eight miles from my home, attending a different high school. We'd met the summer before, teens among a group of twenty who were children of VFW employees hired to pack membership kits for the thousands of veterans across the country. Richard was tall and slender with black, tight curls that frizzed in the Missouri heat. He wore horn-rimmed glasses that gave him a stylishly retro, Buddy Holly look. In class, I often had to force myself to stop thinking about our next date or our last conversation on the phone the night before when I should have been studying. When I knit him a scarf for Christmas, he told me he wrapped it around his chest, tucked it under his pajama shirt and slept with it. How I was able to focus on any of my studies that year I have no idea.

But biology class was important to me. I do remember this: at the end of recitation, when Mr. Stark reached the very last person in class, what I had managed to read the night before fell into place like pieces in a puzzle, all twenty pages or more. My inky notes, with terms tediously copied from the book after talking to Richard, along with the main points outlined, as our teacher had instructed, finally made sense. Mr. Stark was right. I still don't remember what I learned and sincerely wish I could describe the bee dance in detail. What I do recall is the thrill of understanding a complex concept after long work, retracing the path I had just come down, returning to look under each stone of memory.

From the best teachers I think we learn a presence of mind, a kind of integrity—how to take in the world, observe it for our own understanding. In a classroom filled with the smell of formaldehyde, Mr. Stark created a world removed from the tumult of the times: recitation, facts, occasional praise when we struck it right, but no more than that. He guided us through the timeless narrative of nature, beginning with the sun as the source of energy, moving through the biomass—the plant, animal and human kingdoms. He showed us that nature was not removed from who we are, but rested within us, in our capacity to observe, understand and take responsibility for all phases of the natural world: growth, decay, and final chemical absorption into the Earth. One day Mr. Stark asked us, "What is life?" and then immediately provided the answer, finger raised, "Life is a condition." I wrote it in my notebook. I was beginning to see a pattern—life, a condition that always changes. The pattern was not permanent and always in flux.

My biology project, rooted in operant conditioning, was to train mice how to run through a simple cardboard maze I built at home in our basement. Spring was coming, and a project was just what I needed. My relationship with Richard faded when he wanted to take a girl from his journalism class to the end of the year prom. I didn't blame him. When he'd asked me to go, I said I felt too shy attending a prom at his high school rather than mine. I thought he might try to coax me into it, but he didn't. I was heartbroken.

In my experiment, I had three mice. Two were rewarded with a food pellet whenever they took a correct turn in the maze. The other was a control mouse who was never taught how to find its food at the end of the maze. My first interest in behaviorism may have been sparked by a class in which Mr. Stark described Pavlov's experiments with dogs. Also, I remembered reading years before how autistic children like Charlie learned to speak in the article from *Life Magazine* featuring the Lovaas method that used operant conditioning to reward these hard-to-teach children. Why those kids responded so well to operant conditioning intrigued and also dismayed me. If I studied behaviorism, would I understand how someone like my brother thinks? I performed my experiment over about five weeks, dutifully writing up my hypothesis, my methods and observations, but the experiment was tedious and I soon learned that I lacked the discipline to be a scientist.

I also discovered I didn't really like Pavlov or B.F. Skinner and their ideas on how behavior can be manipulated by an outsider. A home-made cardboard maze was not a natural environment for a mouse. And what right did I have in withholding food from an animal? Perhaps my family's initial skepticism about the Lovaas method was spot on. In the last days of my experiment, only one weak mouse remained and I couldn't tell if it was a trial mouse or an experimental mouse. Disease had interfered with the training experience, I concluded. Before school ended, Mr. Stark announced that the snake in the aquarium had to be fed and it preferred live mice. I told my mother I needed to sacrifice my last mouse to the longevity of Mr. Stark's snake. She thought this was a terrible idea and asked me to reconsider, but I carried out my plan, proudly bearing my mouse to Mr. Stark.

What else I remember in those months of falling in love and then losing love was looking into a microscope to gaze at cells within the fine veins of a leaf. I also watched the cells of my own hair seem to tremble. I was told to look for the flexible cell wall and the soft nucleus as it drifted off the slide. With our notebooks open, and eyes focused on the microscope, Mr. Stark taught us how to draw what we see: pencil sharpened with sandpaper, graphite point pressed to the page and never lifted, eyes on the cell appearing on the slide, our sketch lines as detailed as possible. "Notice there are no open lines in nature. All lines are closed," Mr. Stark intoned as he made the rounds to each of us. We were all related to the whole, he was telling us, connected by our condition.

Connected to the Whole

My home state of Michigan, that open-palmed right hand with its prominent thumb was now far away. My brother Charlie lived even further from us than before. Losing my boyfriend Richard was a disappointment, but who I really missed were my brother and grandmother and all my friends on Ferris Street. Those images of people and places were the clear, closed lines of my life.

Now that I was a senior in high school and thinking about college, I realized it might be possible to go back to that land of lakes and pines. I could apply to attend college at the University of Michigan where my father had studied. By the fall of 1971, it had been two and a half years since my family had moved to Kansas City, leaving Michigan behind. I had good grades, was a member of the Honor Society; I had won awards for forensic acting, and volunteered as a tutor for the special education class in my high school. My counselor told me the first thing to do was apply for early acceptance at a safety school, the University of Missouri, about two hours from Kansas City. Once I collected that acceptance, then I could apply for a scholarship to Michigan universities. My counselor thought I had a good chance to receive a scholarship. I remember telling my parents about this plan and hearing no reaction either way from them. I submitted my application in the fall and waited for my acceptance letter. And waited. No word from the University of Missouri. I thought I had been rejected.

Around April, my mother turned to me with a letter in her hand, saying casually, "Oh, this came for you months ago." It was my University of Missouri acceptance letter. I had lost my chance to apply to another school, and as it turned out, had only a few weeks to answer the University of Missouri acceptance without being put on a waiting list. I wanted to go to college, and I wanted to leave my parents' home very badly. Realizing my only exit, I quickly wrote back to the University of Missouri, confirming my intention to attend. My mother looked up from the newspaper she was reading and said I had done the right thing.

Only recently have I been able to understand the context of my mother's action. In a file folder marked "Charlie" that I'd saved after her death, I found a trove of letters she kept about Charlie's institutionalization and care, dating to the time period when I first began to talk about applying to college. My understanding of her stress deepened as I read through these letters. On November 10, 1971, my senior year in high school, my parents received a letter from Fort Custer State Home stating that due to budget restrictions, the institution was "phasing down its resident population," and three-hundred residents, including Charlie, would be transferred to other institutions. This must have been the time of the reported three-minute burn rate of the Fort Custer buildings, although that fact was never stated. Of the seven possible sites Charlie could be sent to, the decision was made to send him to Lapeer State Home. My parents were told to contact A.M. Abuzzo, M.D., the same superintendent interviewed in the documentary from 1962. I remember my mother telling me, in a voice of despair, that Charlie had been transferred by the state of Michigan to Lapeer and she had no say over it.

Another letter dated November 17, 1971 was a typewritten list of all Charlie's possessions with the surprising words "Boarding Home" handwritten below it. These items of clothing included: One ski jacket (in Michigan parlance, a winter coat); nine dress shirts (most likely polo shirts), five pairs of undershorts, one raincoat, three pairs of pajamas, seven pairs of jeans and two suitcases. A form letter dated Nov. 23, 1971 and signed by Dr. Abuzzo, appeals to parents to provide an approval letter from the Social Security Administration so that funds for children in their care could be used. By the notation on the letter in my mother's hand, I am certain my parents were on top of that. They had applied for Social Security benefits years earlier to protect him in case something ever happened to them.

In April of 1972, right around the time my mother handed over my college acceptance letter, my parents received an unusual letter from the Lapeer State Home & Training School, informing them that Charlie was now "ready to return into the community so he can continue developing in accordance with the requirements of our society. His name, therefore, was given to our Community Services Department for the purpose of finding a suitable home which could satisfy his needs." Written at the top of the letter was my mother's clear handwriting: "telephone call made day received". At the bottom she had written: "1. suitable home, 2. special 3. training."

I can imagine my mother trying to piece together what the state of Michigan was planning for her child. First, without her consent, her son had been removed from an institution she trusted to one she despised. She was then notified that he would be transferred from that institution to an unknown home somewhere in Michigan. All of these decisions were made without her knowledge or permission. She had lost control of the care for her child. For a period of time, perhaps many weeks, it was possible my mother didn't know exactly where her son was living. I remember her concern but she shared no specific details. One letter addressed to my parents bluntly states: "I can find no record of his being referred to community placement. When a recommendation is made by those working closely with him that he could better profit by living outside the institution, we will let you know." The extent of Charlie's community placement, from what I can gather by tracing these letters, was a transfer from "building 38" to "building 40."

With time and experience behind me, I've come to understand my mother's mostly unconscious decision to hide my college acceptance letter. She simply didn't want me to attend college out of state, far from her and our home. Under no circumstances was she going to let me apply to a college in Michigan—another child of hers living alone in that state. Yet she was too reticent to tell me how deeply she felt. This is the only explanation I can imagine, years later. And now I can, of course, forgive her this maternal error. If we don't forgive our mothers, who will? In the next year, when I was away in college, my parents would take more assertive control of the changing situation with Charlie's institutionalization and work through both the Michigan and the Missouri social services systems to finally bring him back home. The last letter my parents received was written on new letterhead announcing that the institution had changed superintendents and its name. Oakdale Center for Developmental Disabilities, formerly Lapeer State Home & Training School, was now under the guidance of Albert L. Meuli. The letter states: "Dear Mr. and Mrs. Anderson: This is to inform you that your son was discharged from Oakdale Center for Developmental Disabilities on Monday October 1, 1973 per your request. We are enclosing Charles' Social Security card."

By that evening in October my parents had already met Charlie at the airport where he had flown, accompanied by a social worker, from Detroit to Kansas City. When Charlie took off from the Detroit airport, the weather was the same as it was in Kansas City—cloudy, and in the mid-sixties. Up in the air, my brother traveled the curve of the earth's parabola for three hours to come home. Behind him were eight years in a state institution that he could not describe. Charlie finally landed at the vast one-year-old Kansas City International Airport, sprawling past meadows and farmland of Platte County, much different from the crowded Detroit Metro airport from which he had departed. I was away at college when he arrived. Walking through the airline gate in Kansas City, I was told, he had an irrepressible smile on his face when he saw our mother, father and Bill. In the airport parking lot, before everyone got in the car, my mother looked at Charlie, so tall now, and asked him where he'd been. She said he raised his index finger toward the bright waxing crescent in the early evening sky and shouted, "The moon!"

IV
BEARING A GIFT TO THE WORLD

Two Brothers Washing for Dinner

As the house filled with less and less light, I used to watch them at the sink, their sleeves rolled up ceremoniously—my two brothers washing for dinner. Chattering, the youngest turned the faucet for his older brother who leaned hesitantly forward, reached for soap, then stopped, hands motionless as if they were sculpted mid-air. He was our slow, awkward brother, the one we tried to understand his whole life. He waited for guidance: first warm water, then soap up to the elbows. The youngest knew his brother could not talk back and never would, but when he unfurled a white towel and took his brother's arms to dry, he marveled at their reach—higher, more beyond than his own, his brother's deep, mature muscles and shoulder blades, cutting their long curves. Though he would dream of bearing his older brother like a gift to the world, for now he led him through the hallway of our house, not narrow or dark for long, but reaching an end where a table was set and the candles were burning.

FINDING HOME

While I was away at college, my eleven-year-old brother Bill was the sibling who first bore witness to Charlie's homecoming to Kansas City that fall. He was Charlie's opposite, with blond, hazel-on-the-bluish-side eyes, and a little short for his age. In contrast to Charlie, whose speech still seemed rudimentary, he was highly talkative, conjuring a rich imaginative world inspired by the adventure stories of Darwin setting sail on the *Beagle* for the Galapagos Islands. Bill could turn the whole backyard into his site for discovery. On a morning in July, he found a one-eyed tortoise munching mulberries fallen in abundance by the back fence. The tortoise's beak was stained a deep purple, Bill excitedly pointed out to us, as he lifted it briefly into the air before letting it wander the yard again. He named the tortoise Wiley Post, after the eye-patched aviator.

My brother Bill also once took over the whole first floor of our house on W. 63rd Street. He found old rolls of wallpaper the previous owners had left in the basement and on the reverse side he mapped our neighborhood—every house, and street within a five-block radius, including his elementary school, and all the local stores. He unrolled the wallpaper from the kitchen, showing off his designs as he moved through the dining room, into the living room, up to the front door. He created airplanes from cardboard and glue, and he made himself a chessboard and pieces out of screws, buttons, toothpicks and other spare parts. He tried to share his enthusiasms with Charlie, but just as I realized years ago on Ferris Street, Charlie was difficult to engage in play.

When I was home visiting on a weekend, Bill pulled me by the arm and said, "Hey, come up to my room. Charlie and I want to show you something."

Bill's room was filled with photographs of airplanes and animals, and on one wall, a huge poster of the Beatles. He made Charlie stand right next to it. "OK, Charlie, who's this?" he asked, pointing to the first Beatle, who wore a pair of wire rim glasses.

"George!"

"That's right, Charlie, now who's this?" Charlie gave the correct Beatle's name again, and then again, pronouncing each with precise emphasis. When

Bill came to the guy behind the drums, Charlie shouted "Ringo!" landing on that last vowel as long as he could. Bill was jubilant; he was the person in the family teaching and eliciting Charlie's responses this time. He was the one bearing the gift of our brother, this remarkable person, to the world.

While Charlie was still adjusting to his new life in Kansas City, I was beginning my junior year at the University of Missouri, two hours away in Columbia. The small, one-story house I lived in with two other women during our last two years of college was located on North 8th Street, near the courthouse. A Seventh Day Adventist halfway house was up the block, and across the street an upholstery shop. At the corner drugstore you could purchase a horse bridle or a packet of sassafras-flavored Sen-Sen to cure your bad breath. You could buy your books and ammunition at a ramshackle store across from the courthouse jail. In the spring and early fall, ivy twined through an open space in the window frame and dangled over the bed where I slept and studied. In my large, unruled black notebook, I took notes with a thin-pointed Rapidograph pen that I tended carefully, keeping the small cartridges of ink nestled in my backpack. My handwritten scrawl was almost impossible to read by anyone other than myself, but I remember feeling such fluidity in my thinking, such ease as I jotted down my thoughts. Days and nights in bed facing the street, I read the Modern and Romantic poets, Western and Eastern philosophy, studied French verbs and untwisted German syntax. In my usual headlong collision to reach depth or meaning, I'd stop reading, look out my window, then write on and on, recording thoughts like this, I'm embarrassed to admit, "No matter of consequence, this life. It ends. We dream. It ends again." As much as Charlie's homecoming was a celebration in my family, I must have felt anxious about what the future would hold for me and my family members.

My brother Bill had experienced a serious illness two weeks before I entered college in the late summer of 1972. At the time I was still worried he would die. Although he recovered quickly and has never again had difficulties with this syndrome, I couldn't erase the visual image of my little brother carried out the backdoor by my mother and father to the hospital. During my years in college, I became obsessed with the idea that my brother's illness would return. When I was at home for a visit, I would wake up in the middle of the night just to check his breathing, very much like a mother. The doctors didn't know what caused Charlie's disability or my childhood migraines, my mother told me, and they didn't know what had happened to Bill. In short, doctors didn't know much about the body or the brain. My mother advised again, as she would often, that I forgo motherhood as our family was vulnerable to frightening illnesses. I didn't question her caution at the time and she offered no other alternative or expectation for me as I entered into a new phase of young adulthood.

As the fragile line between life and death began to haunt me, I once again turned to the written word. With my great aunt's graduation gift of fifteen dollars, I bought the *Norton Anthology of Modern Poetry*, filled with poets I've carried with me my whole life: Whitman, Dickinson, Rich, Levertov, Merwin, and many more. In addition to poetry, I was also reading French and German philosophy ravenously, trying to unpack my anxiety, and trying desperately to get further away from my parents' pessimism. My readings of existentialism and its close twin, phenomenology, seemed to tame my obsessive anxieties. One writer I discovered was Maurice Merleau-Ponty whose languorous phrases helped to clarify many of my angst-heavy questions about life, survival and the randomness of death. "Neither my birth nor my death can appear to me as experiences of my own. . . I know that people are born and die, but I cannot know my own birth and death," I copied in my notebook from his *Phenomenology of Perception*. His words reminded me of our high school biology lesson that life was a condition caught in time. Our lives at the end may pass into the nothingness of the universe, yet we possess the gift of attention, perceiving the present in all its beauty and sorrow. Merleau-Ponty's words enchanted because I trusted the cold stone of their assertions, smooth as marble, which paradoxically has the feel of softness.

The kind administrators at the University of Missouri let me design my own course of study by the time I was a junior in 1974: philosophy, languages and poetry, toward a Bachelor of General Studies. I was preparing myself for a career in writing. I began my pursuit by studying feverishly not only to quell my anxieties, but to learn how to channel my imagination while at the same time lead an engaged life. I don't think I was equipped to grasp the full intent of Merleau-Ponty or the other phenomenologists, but what I did absorb cast a laser light on my own path of study. Contemporary philosophy with its emphasis on language and perception interested me because I thought it might answer questions I had about the communication differences of my silent, smiling brother, or at least help me imagine what it was like to be in the mind of someone so different. I was also beginning the intimate, delicate work of writing poems, a practice that demands intense introspection but also a Zen-like attention to life in the moment.

On Charlie's first Thanksgiving home in 1973, my mother showed him how to lay a plate, knife, fork and napkin on the dining room table. As we all watched, he took over, and with each plate he set down he repeated our names: "Cathy, Mummer, Daddy, Billy" in a slow ritual that obviously gave him pleasure. While we watched, my family realized how happy he was to be with us at Thanksgiving, the first time in years. We were equally thrilled he was pronouncing everyone's name with such attention and care, a sign that he could communicate with and respond to the world around him. As he spent more time with us, Charlie was starting to demonstrate a breadth of language beyond his deliberate naming of family members. He was beginning to converse in a limited dialog that was more expressive and animated. Soon we'd ask him to name anything that came to mind—setting photographs or unusual objects in front of him, anticipating his pronouncements. We all felt as if we were witnessing Adam first name the animals, so earnest was he in his precision, with one finger in the air as the words jumbled forth. The words Charlie accrued very rapidly were mostly these concrete nouns, demonstrating what Dehaene has described as the continued plasticity of an adult's brain to acquire new vocabulary. This was a very creative time for my brother—he was out of the institution, living in a group home and working in a sheltered workshop, all experiences that helped him acquire more language. The settings where his language was most robust were these small gatherings with his family or roommates. Although echolalia still seemed to be the dominant way he engaged in conversation, it was accepted and understood. Charlie was also learning how to tell jokes, a sign that he really was part of the family again. When you pointed to a lettuce leaf and asked him what color it was, he'd shout, "Blue!" and then crack up laughing.

Like a poet, each approach my brother made in language was a new beginning as he found the words to present his perceptions. In his book *Poetry as Survival*, poet Gregory Orr relates the story of the German poet Gunter Eich who felt the need to create a new language after the devastation of World War II. In the face of this reality, the poet chose to write first primarily in nouns, to establish his orientation to a new world. Interestingly, the German word for nouns can be translated as "thing-words." Eich states in a lecture from that time, "Real language is the falling together of the word and the object." This falling together for my brother was also sensory, an orientation since childhood that stayed with him his whole life—colors, tastes, sounds, shapes. My brother's habit of raising a finger before he spoke revealed how tactile the physical act of utterance was for him. Orr further quotes Roland Barthes in a revelatory description of how language feels when we use it. I wonder if my brother felt this way: "Language is a skin. I rub my language against the other. It is as if I had words instead of fingers, or fingers at the tip of my words."

After living with our family for months, Charlie was settled into a community group home where he had roommates and a job. The medication then prescribed for him, Mellaril (or thioridazine, HCI), could cause the involuntary movements of tardive dyskinesia, but at the time it was the only medication that seemed to calm him. My mother and father believed that without this powerful antipsychotic drug, Charlie, whose outbursts of frustration sometimes frightened people, would not be able to adapt to community living or a sheltered workshop, a community program in light industry where participants earned a salary based on piece-rate production.

I grew to question the safety of this medication, but my parents always maintained it was worth the risk. Throughout the years Charlie had to be closely monitored to make sure he was not showing signs of tardive dyskinesia. The only obvious side effect noticed at first was a little weight gain. After a visit home, I wrote in my black notebook, "Charlie is so sweet when I first meet him. He looks directly at me, following my words with his eyes, then he drifts off, but it is pleasant, if only for a few seconds." At the end of this brief description, I note: "He is getting plump."

Charlie and I were acquiring our education in very different ways, and once again in separate cities, each of us passing through a narrow threshold of development that would carry us into adulthood. This liminal phase, marked by what poet Jane Hirshfield calls "a threshold state of ambiguity, openness and indeterminacy" would never be duplicated and built the foundation of our lives. It's a passage that prepares a young person for the demands of adulthood, common for many families, even ours, though I didn't see it that way at the time. Looking back, I realize my brother and I were not so unique, after all. Because Charlie's transition was different from mine—he was released from an institution while I was graduated from high school and sent to college—I only saw the features that made him unusual and our family odd.

With Charlie's arrival back home, I thought of our family and the experiences of Charlie's institutionalization with sadness. I quietly told only my close friends about the institution, ashamed as I was about my family's responsibility, and indirectly, my own, for placing him in Fort Custer the length of his childhood. What did my parents perceive in Charlie's behavior that I needed protection from? Why couldn't he have lived with us? Why were we not strong enough, unselfish enough, to make changes to our living arrangements, to accommodate him? The only answer I could come up with was that for many reasons, my family could not, over the course of eight years, succeed in offering a childhood home for Charlie who needed so much constant care. Yet, paradoxically here he was, transplanted back to his family and community, becoming enriched by a vivid period of growth and transition.

At this point in Charlie's development, my family accepted his disabilities with a growing optimism about how he could live in our community. My mother and I still believed autism was the best description for Charlie's condition. However, this word was not used yet in discussions of his care and not understood by the general public. To my mother and me, this ambiguity allowed a glimmer of hope; perhaps through growing research more would be known about autism that could help him. And Charlie was still developing. Not only was he rapidly acquiring more words than he would at any time in life, he was experiencing joys denied him in an institutional setting, what young adults do spontaneously: play sports, music, eat junk food, joke with roommates. A photograph I love shows Charlie lean and tanned with a mop of shaggy brown hair as he rollicks with his group home roommates playing bumper cars, just like any young person. New sensations and sounds must have come at him in a tumble: names for people, things he used in his sheltered-workshop job, places he was going to visit. I was fascinated by how he was acquiring new words so rapidly, and still mystified by the gaps in his capacity to communicate.

Everyone is familiar with the strange, "tip of the tongue" feeling in which a word is locked within us, trying to get free. This temporary state was, to my best guess (as someone who is neurotypical), what my brother felt all the time when we pushed him to communicate. When asked, he could hesitantly and slowly recite back important information like his address and phone number. His receptive vocabulary was large and growing, but his spoken language, requiring initiative, needed constant prompting and training. Unchanged since the days when my mother first taught him to speak were the persistent echolalic responses he uttered, as well as his reluctance to initiate conversation.

He still gave the impression that he had no sense of an "I." To me, it was as if Charlie could not see himself as separate from his own perceptions. His understanding of the world seemed to be based purely on how he perceived it, and not as a separate "I" acting with self-agency. I found it fascinating, though again, I am someone who is neurotypical.

In those early years, before I understood the clinical terms for Charlie's communication differences, and as I was beginning to understand his style of communication beyond the use of words, I felt a parallel between the struggle he made in speaking to the efforts I made in writing. Charlie's hesitations in finding words, his preference to echo back words, and to shun using an "I" was for me an opening to understanding the nuances of poetic language in a number of ways. When he had to, my brother used halting words to ask for water or food, or to yell for the dog to get out of his chair. Even more pointedly, his facial expressions showed joy or apprehension. His bodily movements reflected his feelings of curiosity, expectation or frustration. There was dignity in his spare utterances and in the communicative silence of his body language. In poetry, bringing words out of silence and into consciousness is also a struggle. If you go too far with description or explanation, you miss conveying the transcendent meaning of your true intention. As Wittgenstein once stated, "There are, indeed, things that cannot be put into words. They are what is mystical." I believed this unspoken connection my brother had with me and others went beyond language and entered the realm of beauty and the poetic. I also realized there were limits to these presumptions of mine. I could never really know how Charlie saw himself in the world because he couldn't tell me. I could only perceive a glimpse of his world, its beauty, or its irritation, its presence or uncertainty. This ambiguity created a bond between us, and in that way, I consider my brother to be my first teacher in the art of poetry.

At a Threshold

The university I attended was the major institution of higher education in the state with a medical school, agricultural school and journalism school, yet Columbia always struck me as a town set in an anxious, cold war time warp. Despite its caught-in-amber feel, the city was experiencing the same changes as the rest of the country. The U.S. was in flux: the slow ending of the decade-old Vietnam War, the attacks on anti-war marchers that preceded that ending, an authoritarian Nixon White House in the early 70s, in addition to the subsequent Watergate scandal. The establishment was losing credibility, opening the inevitable but real questioning of the generation that came before us. Our generation grew up in the shadow of the atomic bomb, with its emphasis on paranoia and survival tactics and its neglect of social problems. It was clear that the War on Poverty of the 1960s—too brief and not targeted—was lost in America. My father, a journalist who made his career documenting the postwar experience, was someone who influenced my thinking yet also became the target of my rebellion. Our bickering was constant. When I was home in the fall of my junior year, he saw a book by Friedrich Nietzsche in my backpack and announced that he would no longer pay for my college expenses if I continued to study a writer who inspired the Nazis. I was shocked to hear he thought this possible and not sure where his paranoia originated. I challenged his bluff by telling him I would now pay for my own schooling.

I learned, too, that women were now gaining reproductive rights for the first time. That fact alone may have set my father off-kilter, though he would never broach the subject. If we wanted, even as students, we could obtain birth control pills for a sliding scale fee at an off-campus clinic. These cultural transformations were changing what we thought of our deepest selves, propelling us toward an idea of freedom Jean Paul Sartre and Simone de Beauvoir would have applauded. Many nights I would stay up late with my two roommates, Dena and Michelle, burning our sandalwood candles and drinking coffee mixed with cream and Kahlua as we discussed questions launched from lectures we attended by Germaine Greer or Angela Davis. I can't remember exactly what we said, but I know our late-night conversations revolved around questions such as "What is our identity now as women with a career beyond making a home?" or "How are we going to make a positive change in the world after the mistake of the Vietnam War?" To us, middle-class culture, with its traditional expectations of women, and all its privileges and prisons, was up for revision. The three of us assumed we would be earning our own incomes, making our own decisions, yet underlying our existential search was another question: "How do I make a living doing what I love?" We were students of our time and place; we were becoming humanists. I expected to teach and write; Michelle was preparing for medical school and Dena for a career as a clinical psychologist.

In early October of 1974, a young woman turned to me as we both walked out of our class on Modern Poetry and asked, "Did you hear that Anne Sexton killed herself?" Anne Sexton's death: a hose, a closed garage, a running car. I knew what she meant: first Sylvia Plath and now Anne Sexton. Who could we learn from? Anne Sexton wrote compulsively of her own suicide attempts, and of death's blunt facts either in the abstract or in the textured nuances of grief, as in "The Truth the Dead Know:"

> And what of the dead? They lie without shoes
> in their stone boats.
> They are more like stone
> than the sea would be if it stopped. They refuse
> to be blessed, throat, eye and knucklebone.

These lines were too austere for my reckoning when I read them at the age of twenty. Now, I admire the restraint of this poem, the renunciation of any attempt to understand, love, or even forgive. Anne Sexton permits no comfort in this bare telling. "The truth the dead know," but the dead keep silent.

That day I learned of Anne Sexton's suicide, I looked up her biography in my *Norton Anthology of Modern Poetry* and was startled to realize she shared the same birthdate as my mother: November 9, 1928. I began to have a persistent, reoccurring dream that my mother was telling me she wanted to kill herself. The dream went something like this: We're talking together in a kitchen on a cloudy day. We live in a high-rise above a maze of traffic and noise below. I try everything I can to convince her not to do it. Later, we're driving through the same unknown, gray and crowded city, weaving an old car through a canyon of tall skyscrapers. It's not clear who is at the wheel. I'm still trying to talk my mother out of committing suicide. In the quirky bend of dream space, I look up as we drive by the building where we live and realize my mother has plunged to her death, even though I had just seen her in the car, sitting next to me, talking.

It's not surprising that in my dream I conflated the fatal depression of Anne Sexton with my mother's feelings of loss and inadequacy as the mother of Charlie. She often confided those feelings to me, and often they were a burden. Her insistence that I never have children was startling each time she said it, though I knew her intentions were good. In the kitchen, alone with my mother, I often played the reluctant therapist.

My mother would not die for another twenty-five years, but hers was an addict's gamble against death in many ways—she was a nonstop smoker and died of lung cancer. A therapist told me that my mother had committed what she called "slow suicide by nicotine." Not quite the case. My mother was much more complex and alive than that. She loved us, she loved people and as difficult as it was, she loved the life she was given. I think it must have been the same for Anne Sexton. Years later, I met a few poets who knew Anne personally—women who studied with her, benefited from her generous critique and solid praise. Another friend of mine who also knew these women once told me that whenever the name of Anne Sexton came up, they found themselves in a room lit with grief.

In searching for women poets to emulate, the most absorbing voices I found—Adrienne Rich, Sylvia Plath, Denise Levertov—were also the ones who still seemed, like Anne Sexton, far removed from my experience. My peers and I were not walking into the lives of the mothers who preceded us: at graduation, we were not marrying right away and we were not going back home. We were trying to carve a path out of our talents, and we were upending a lot of tradition. In a way, we felt like we were taking on roles that had been reserved for men. I remember asking Louise Glück, at her reading at the University of Missouri, if she thought it was all right for a female poet to write in a male voice, what I found myself frequently doing. She said, "Why not?" and "Remember Yeats's Crazy Jane poems in a female voice?" I continued a long journey navigating through the literature of male voices, and then female ones, until coming to realize how little the gender of a poet mattered to me. Poet Marianne Boruch has said that when she writes, she enters a space that is neither male nor female, but a transcendent state. How a woman makes a life of writing is another story altogether.

To pay for my college and living expenses, I added extra hours to my job as a desk clerk at the Downtown Motor Inn on Broadway in Columbia and stretched the generous check of one thousand dollars given me by my great-aunt Gladys. Walking down Broadway I wore my mother's first winter coat when she moved with my father from Florida to Michigan in the 1950s. It was suede, the color of burnt leaves and flared in the wind. At my throat I wore touches of lavender and patchouli oil from a small dark vial. I've saved the vial, now less than an eighth full but on opening, still as fragrant as those days I can usher back in one quick inhalation. If I was going to be a writer, I decided, I needed to replace my flimsy typewriter and buy that sturdy black Underwood I'd seen in the used goods store on the next block. I remember waving to the owner's grandson, wrapped in a body cast and propped in a chair set in the front window so he could watch people passing by on the street. The little boy had just survived being hit by a car the week before. My new typewriter was less than twenty dollars.

My bedroom with the twining ivy was a converted side-porch with a gas heater and a curtain to separate it from the kitchen. In the winter, I'd wake to find a layer of frost crusted on my blanket as I got up quick to light the gas heater with the name Warm Morning emblazoned on the side. When an old tree fell in the front yard, missing the roof but covering the whole house, my roommates and I stepped around its flowing branches and leaves for weeks as if the tree had become another room. People came by from miles around to view the tree and wish us well. When Bill Minor, the compact Downtowner handyman who could fix anything, was released after a spell in the hospital, we invited him for lasagna at our home on North 8th Street. Michelle and I moved the round wooden table to the center of the living room and set out wine glasses and cloth napkins. In Columbia, the three of us had found a community to last the next few years, the best kind, sprouting with ease from our daily comings and goings with people who didn't resemble us in age or experience.

One night at the Downtowner, I looked up from reading to see the architect Buckminster Fuller at the front desk, ready to be checked in. He was to be a speaker the next day at a conference on energy-efficient design. The restaurant was closed but I pointed to the late-hour donut shop across the street. Guessing he might be interested to learn more about Columbia,

I had the urge to show him this neat trick: if you tilted your head a bit and looked west on Broadway, you could make out the image of Donald Duck in the streetlight pattern. I thought better and went back to reading William Wordsworth for my course on the British Romantics. On another night, three Shriners sped through the lobby on scooters, just long enough to twist a long red balloon into the shape of a wiener dog before they honked away. That must have been the night I drew a black-inked cartoon titled "Portrait of the Artist as a Young Desk" on the back of a Downtowner Motor Inn check-in registration form and taped it to the switchboard. In the spring, I learned about frog hunting along the Missouri River from a retired doorman named Mr. Mercy, who promised that if he ever saw me on a Columbia street corner, he'd walk right up to say "Hello, Downtowner." And I'd know to answer back the same.

In a photograph I've saved, Bill Minor is sitting with his cap and navy-blue jacket on, legs apart, head tilted to one side as if he were announcing, as he often did, "I'm fixing soon to get me some hobo eats." In the background is the wood paneling of 1970s hotel décor, and next to him is the switchboard of the front desk, with its array of levers and buttons. Bill was getting the rooms ready for a conference on, of all things, phenomenology, sponsored by the philosophy department at the University of Missouri. His job was to put a "Welcome Phenomenologists" sign up on the Downtowner Motor Inn marquee, above the medallion-shaped yellow crown that overlooked Broadway. John Studer, the night clerk who sported a thin mustache and a pistol, admitted that he too didn't know how to pronounce or spell "phenomenologists." With delight I wrote out that long word for Bill to refer to when he climbed the ladder to set up the letters on the marquee. On the sign board by the front desk was a bullet hole no one had repaired years ago when the hotel was robbed. Underneath it, I added plastic letters to create another welcome sign for the phenomenologists. Then I waited for them to come through the doors of the Downtowner.

Written on the back of another square registration card are notes I made when reading Alfred Schutz's *The Phenomenology of the Social World* for my course on phenomenology: "Problem: so many 'thous,' cannot bring each into relationship." And in the margins of Schutz's last chapter, "Problems of Interpretive Sociology," I'd written: "we have immediate awareness of the Other, but of ourselves, only in retrospect." Whether I was overwhelmed with the prospect of many unknown doors beginning to open for me, or continually perplexed, as I always would be, by the difficulty of connecting to my brother Charlie, it's hard to say. I know at the time I wrote poem drafts in my notebook about watching the back of a lover's head recede into the night, and another about the impossibility of understanding my mother as much as I tried to cross the bridge of her nose deep into her eyes. My journal entries were hesitations, hedges, an approach to understanding the "Other," perpetually escaping or fading, a "thou" refusing integration. They were also about failure, a topic I presumed to know at the age of twenty-one. Amidst all this darkness, my inky notebooks also contained sketches of tomatoes and beans in plans for a garden with the neighbor's broken Volvo in the center of the page. One day toward the end of my senior year, I realized I'd lost my Rapidograph pen, fallen out of my backpack into the street as I dashed to a class. I'll never own one like that again, I thought, and then in an instant, told myself I didn't need it anymore. I would strike out on my own as a writer, using the tools I found as I went along.

To say my brother's unique way of communicating taught me how to write poetry may seem like a leap—sentimental or exaggerated—but I mean the echoing speech and the gestures he used as his own form of language resembled a whole gestalt of expression. In a poem, words are brought forth from a space deep inside, one that comes before language. Poetry reveals the loneliness of a speaker, the aimless strike in the air, the risk of being ignored or forgotten. In watching Charlie develop at this point in his life, opening his mouth with hesitation to speak to our family and others in a voice that may or may not be understood, I realized his long achievement and the hope it offered. His words, gestures and quiet presence were his insistence on being known in a world that was not used to seeing people like him. Let's say he taught me what I needed at the time. My brother had grown into a brave young man and his bravery made me stronger.

Into the World

One of the bravest things I saw Charlie do was sign his name to a paycheck and cash it at the grocery store. It must have been in the late 1970s after he started living in a group home and working at a sheltered workshop where he and other people with intellectual disabilities packed boxes, attached labels to mail, and performed other light tasks. He was paid per piece of completed work, and because his production was slow, his paycheck was usually not more than twenty-five dollars per month. This was his money to spend on treats like candy or soda pop. My mother and I were with him at the local grocery store on a busy Friday evening, and I had just come home for a holiday visit. As we waited in line at the service counter, my mother said, "this will take a while." She directed Charlie to the side, helped him find his state issued I.D. and pull out the curled paycheck from his pocket. The cashier offered him a pen and patiently waited as he climbed the mountain of his long name, Charles Anderson, printing it out in large block letters at the bottom line of the check. She counted the twenty-five dollars into his hand and my mother helped him put it back into his wallet and then his pocket. People gathered behind us, but no one hurried him. He was regarded with the same respect and attention paid to any adult in a public space. I was very proud of him that evening.

My brother's eight years of childhood in the institution was time lost we could never recover. On his return home we knew that by encouraging him to speak, look people in the eye, and master the skills he possessed in neatness and motor dexterity, a better life could open up for him. We were getting used to the idea that my brother could find a niche, despite the accelerated American work culture surrounding him. As a family, we seemed to have traveled from relying on the frightening generalities of the myth of his birth and disability to the daily specifics of his life. And our Kansas City community was growing to accept Charlie as he was. Charlie's inherent soul, his personality and depth as a person were coming into focus.

By the late 1970s I was living in the cold and rough-hewn city of Syracuse for graduate study. Although I tried to keep in touch, I didn't see my brother on a regular basis. I missed him, and often tried to imagine his new life in the group home, at the sheltered workshop, and with my family. At this time, Charlie, along with thousands in his cohort, was making a transition, a first in history, from the institution to community living. The explicit rules of the institution from which he came were created for protection—the institution's liability, and also my brother's safety. The historical purpose of institutionalization has always been to provide that dual safety purpose, the protection of the residents from the community and the community from the residents. Charlie's life now would be much kinder, more embracing, yet sometimes as with anything new, there were collisions along the way.

Once, in a phone call, my mother told me about a woman who tried to prevent Charlie and other group home members from riding a local school bus. The bus followed a rural route from the group home to the sheltered workshop and was easy to catch. The woman claimed Charlie and his roommates were too old to ride a school bus with children on board. The mother felt they would scare the elementary school children. Charlie was tall and husky, he stepped on the bus too fast, and he didn't speak clearly. Charlie's roommates were too loud when they talked. She took her complaint to court. I don't recall the details, only my mother's fear Charlie could be barred from accessing a public amenity, the way he had not been permitted to attend public school as a child. She and my father had to testify about Charlie's disabilities, his temperament and how he was supervised. Eventually the problem was solved when the city implemented a transportation service for people with disabilities across the metro area. This solution recognized the needs of people who had before been excluded from public life. My parents were relieved.

For Charlie to live safely in the world, he had to be evaluated psychologically, behaviorally and medically throughout his life. He needed the protection of a guardian—my father—named by probate court in Kansas City. Years later, after my father died, I would assume that responsibility. This designation and the medical and psychological evaluations created their own strict set of expectations, easily recognized as I looked back over the paperwork from forty years ago. One early and well-written evaluation of Charlie for placement in a Kansas City group home and sheltered workshop was fascinating to me because it revealed how others saw him when I was living far away and not witness to this phase of his life. The full report is revealing in many ways:

Charles is pleasant and generally cooperative in the classroom. He does anything he is asked to do if he is capable. He possesses all self-help skills. He interacts only slightly with his peers. He seems to participate and interact if he is encouraged to do so but will not initiate conversations or activities. He does not seem to be withdrawn but appears to be shy. He tends to be somewhat echolalic, but does have some speech. No destruction of property has been noted at this time.

Charles can adapt to a routine fairly well. He picks up and returns his check sheet each day in class, keeps his desk neat, and performs his daily tasks. He can count methodically but has no concept of number meaning. He can print his name but cannot copy from the blackboard. He has no reading skills and does not always recognize survival terms such as men and women. He may, at times, use the women's restroom. Charles can sort colors, use scissors and can draw. He likes art. Charles can perform many types of fine motor activities.

It's clear the tasks my brother mastered at Fort Custer put him ahead when it came to community living. He passed the tests, allowing him to live in group homes with other young men his age and to work in a sheltered workshop. He would not cause damage to property, thus protecting others from him, the evaluator thought important enough to note. Presumably, he could also be trained to use the right restroom. However, year after year into the mid-1980s, my brother's glowing evaluations always ended with a diagnosis that felt like a square peg pushed into a round hole: "Severe to profound mental retardation." He was often seen as a permanent patient, a young man with an IQ of 40. This assumed my brother had no interior thought process, or very little. One evaluator mentioned Charlie didn't show any particular interest in girls, but I knew this was probably an oversight. He was very shy when he met my female friends, an indication of intimate feelings he was unable to socially express. In one evaluation, the observer first noted my brother's neatness, dexterity and fine motor skills and then asserted that these same attributes worked against him, causing him to move too slowly, become hesitant, and not initiate or solve problems. Damned if you do, damned if you don't. Charlie's speech was noted, repeatedly, as "difficulty in communicating, with rapid and pushed speech."

For someone like my brother with intellectual disabilities, communication disorders and autism, mental health was always foreground. It defined his public face. He could conduct no action in the public sphere without his disability revealing itself, either in his gait, his slowness to respond to a traffic walk light, or in his inability to speak to a cashier. Like so many social constructs such as race and disability, the role of cognition in someone's life is dependent on the era in which it is defined. And in a culture such as ours in which judgments—positive or negative—are made at lightning speed based on the person's visual appearance, my brother was totally dependent on the assessment of strangers.

When Charlie attended St. Mary's Episcopal church in downtown Kansas City with my parents (they too had left the Catholic church), his diagnosis didn't matter. The three of them entered through large wooden doors where they were welcomed by warm, church-going faces. Charlie, dressed up in a suit and tie, returned their greetings with his own chirpy hello. When everyone stood up to sing, Charlie followed. When they bowed their heads in prayer, he did the same, adding to the murmur in the pews. When my mother thumbed the hymnal to find the right number, he picked up his and made sure it was open to the exact same page. Later, at coffee hour, Charlie would forego conversation and head straight for the brightly iced cookies. He did well in an otherwise dog-eat-dog world, his attention narrowed to the most essential: the names of his family and roommates, the food he liked and colors that delighted him. What more did a person need? He had found a place, a community.

While I was living on the East Coast, far from home and my brother, I often thought about the children I saw at Fort Custer, such as the little boy who built the haphazard chair. What happened to him and others like him who were most likely now living in the community? Whenever I met someone new, either a co-worker, friend, or even potential romantic partner, I told them pretty quickly I had a brother with intellectual disabilities who had grown up in an institution. The mainstream advice was to introduce this information slowly, so the person could get to know you first. As if they needed an inoculation against this disturbing news! Such advice reminded me of my parents' instructions when I was a child, "to keep quiet about Charlie," reason enough for defiance. I introduced myself as the sister of a man on the autistic spectrum as a way to seek out other siblings, friends and relatives of people with disabilities. I wanted to know if others had similar experiences as mine growing up with a sibling with intellectual disabilities and autistic traits. It was lonely out there.

At Syracuse University I held the Cornelia C. Ward Fellowship in poetry from 1976-1977. With the fellowship came enormous expectations I realized early on I could not fulfill. I lived on the third floor of a nineteenth-century house high up on Comstock Ave. The apartment was uninsulated, truly an artist's garret where my roommate and I spent the winter wrapped in wool blankets. During one hard winter storm, the window over my desk shattered as I was studying. I just missed the shards flying all over the room. Most days were sunless and cold, as was the graduate school atmosphere. After a poetry workshop in the afternoon, I would take a bus down West Onandoga Street to an old neighborhood where a young woman I'll call Claire lived in a group home with other women who had intellectual disabilities. Lonely and tired of academia, I'd volunteered through a city agency to be Claire's friend, to help her engage in conversation. I wanted to see how people like Charlie were adjusting after so many institutions had closed, and how they were learning new skills. I was far away from home where Charlie was making his adjustment, and I wanted to know more about what life in a group home was like.

Claire was quiet when I talked with her on the couch in a living room with high ceilings and no other furniture. I'd ask her the same things I'd ask Charlie—what she did during the day, what she had for breakfast, what she liked to do for fun. She would answer shyly. I was misled by her perfectly formed speech and assumed she would tell me more, but she preferred not. We looked at her photo album and a few fashion magazines I had brought with me. On the phone a few days before, her case worker told me Claire's father had died recently. In response, Claire had moved all her possessions out of her room, placing sweaters, pants, and stuffed animals in paper grocery bags. About eight of them lined the hallway in front of her upstairs bedroom. The case worker didn't understand why Claire had done this. She wanted me to find out. I didn't know how to do that and thought questioning her would be intrusive. Claire was in grief. I was her friend. What I could offer was just to sit and be with her.

When my graduate exam at Syracuse came up in the spring, I froze and walked out of the room, telling my long-distance friends the exam was a soulless exercise in rote memorization. I was only partly right. I froze because I'd paid too much attention to William Blake's cosmology and not enough to the plot lines of Jane Austen. The stress of taking a test in a room crowded with other nervous people reminded me too much of the stand and deliver days of Catholic school. What did I learn from this failure? Unlike grade school, punishment wasn't coming. No one judged me. Just like Charlie, I wasn't perfect and didn't have to be. With that embarrassment behind me, I took up bartending at another hotel and the next fall moved to Storrs, Connecticut where Dena was in graduate school, and where I became her roommate again. Not long after my move, I realized a master's degree would be valuable as a teacher in English, and I spent the next nine months working various jobs in Storrs and nearby Willimantic while studying to retake the exam. That spring Syracuse University generously let me take it through a proctor at the University of Connecticut. I passed easily, submitted my creative thesis, and finally earned a Master's degree in English.

More than once during those months in Connecticut the unexpected happened. I gained writing experience by working as a stringer for a daily paper, *The Willimantic Chronicle,* where I was paid by the word for published stories about that rural Connecticut area. The rate increased when a story appeared on the front page, and a number of my stories made it in. I had to quit, though, when I damaged my car on the way to the newspaper office in the early morning after staying up all night to finish a story on a contentious town council vote. I had no money to get it fixed and needed a job I could get to by hitching or borrowing Dena's car. In January, I found a job not too far away as an aide in a local school program for developmentally disabled children. That was my chance to work with an extraordinary teacher, Eileen Fucile, a native of the Boston area, and a dedicated specialist in difficult cases of adjustment for kids with intellectual disabilities. Her breadth of knowledge of autism and intellectual disabilities impressed me deeply, along with her quick wit and curiosity about how children learned. I knew that from Eileen I could pick up a few ideas to help Charlie's development.

Eileen was the lead teacher for two young girls, one who had Down Syndrome, a six-year-old I'll call Maddie, and another eight-year-old girl I'll call Lonnie who was on the autistic spectrum. Neither Maddie nor Lonnie had language or social skills, and both needed twenty-four-hour help with feeding, toileting, getting dressed and overall supervision. Eileen and I were a good match for these girls—she had a sister with Down Syndrome, and I had Charlie. In Eileen's classroom, work began the minute the child came through the door. This was no mean feat. Maddie was usually flying around the room, eager to scatter toys or roll along on the carpeted floor, throwing her whole body into the action. Lonnie felt at home jumping up and down, waving her hands, and dancing in her own parade. Both girls ignored each other. I had no idea how to get the children to focus. Eileen, however, knew better than to convey defeat or negativism. Instead, she showed the purest delight in their presence, patiently steering them toward a routine that would takes months to instill.

Eileen decided the girls would learn to color. I didn't believe this would be possible. Both girls screamed, fussed and tried to slip out of their chairs repeatedly when we set them down with crayons and paper. I remembered Charlie's haphazard mastery of crayons when we were kids and my disappointment in him. These were different children, I realized, and the stakes were higher. If the girls could calm down for more than a few minutes they might be able to attend a regular classroom. Eileen taught me how to gently move a girl's hand over the paper, in spite of the protests, yelling and real tears. The reward for each child's gradual cooperation was based on what they liked to do. For Lonnie, it was to run around the room. For Maddie, it was time to cuddle with a fluffy toy kitten. We both worked with the girls, month after month. Unbelievably, by the end of the school term, they were each sitting down by themselves and picking up crayons to color on manilla paper! This activity, on the surface such a small accomplishment, meant both girls would have a much better chance in school and in their communities. They were finding a place in a world that would not have accepted them decades earlier.

In the 1970s through the 1980s as more people with intellectual disabilities entered the mainstream, practices were slowly becoming more humane and person-centered, rather than focused on liability and security. The groundwork was most definitely laid by educators like Eileen as well as the parents of children with intellectual disabilities. These gradual changes also occurred because a cadre of sympathetic mental health workers, caregivers, psychologists, and educators were finding the language to understand minds so different from the mainstream. They were thinking out of the box, engaging with parents, and also asking questions of people with intellectual disabilities. Rosemary F. Dybwad of Brandeis University's Heller School for Advanced Studies in Social Work, an admired advocate for people with intellectual disabilities, once summed up the time period:

> *People with severe—and that means obvious and visible—*
> *disabilities are moving freely through the community, [where*
> *they] shop in the supermarkets, ride the buses and increasingly the*
> *airplanes, visit the beaches, and attend movies and ball games;*
> *and they are doing this as individuals, not in large labeled groups.*

It is hard to imagine now that these activities would have been remarkable, but in 1985, when this description was written, they were.

Over time my brother's terse, judgmental evaluations began to change, becoming more holistic, re-titled in 1996 as an "Individual Habitation Plan," with an emphasis on identifying skills he could further develop, such as speech and an understanding of money. My parents were beginning to feel less anxious when he met people in public. However, there were times when I could tell Charlie's entry into adulthood was painful for my mother. These were brief glimpses. Once, Dena came by my house a few days after Christmas to pick me up for a night out. Dena was one of Charlie's favorite people. When she saw him, she shook off the snow on her boots and rushed to give him a hug. Dena's brother came in the house, too, a tall, dark-haired, handsome young man now attending college in Columbia. I introduced him to Charlie, and then to my mother. In a glance I could tell my mother realized what I did: Dena's brother's good looks resembled Charlie's, who was about his same age. In her face, for a brief moment, I could see a fleeting sorrow. I never talked to her about that moment, but I've never forgotten it.

We were lucky Charlie showed so much enthusiasm for learning in group homes and sheltered workshops where he was placed. With great pride, my parents often told me about evaluation meetings with a social worker, group home manager or sheltered workshop supervisor. Charlie had grown and improved, and most significantly, his evaluators now saw him in a positive light and felt he was making a contribution to his household and doing well at his sheltered workshop job. He was proud of that monthly paycheck, yet he never fully mastered the concept of money, often standing up at a restaurant to helpfully throw away the green bills he mistook for trash. It didn't matter. My mother started to refer to him as "Charles," the name on his birth certificate and what he was called by his sheltered workshop supervisor and in his formal evaluations. I think my mother used Charles in recognition of his adulthood, as a way to respect his autonomy, an echo of who he was now in the wider culture. This was a brave act on her part, to let my brother go, allow him to grow into adulthood. I admired her so much for that. But Charles was a name I never got used to and I would call him Charlie throughout his life. To me, that name underscored my connection to him as a person I had known since the earliest days of our childhood. I've always liked the bright ring of it.

Rooms on Paseo Boulevard

One morning I saw where they slept, under plaid or flowered coverlets, one bed beside the other, deep within the rooms of the old house on Paseo. Their towels hung on a rack by the sink, each man's name inked at the edge. I could see how their white sheets whipped in the air as their beds were made as if the men who had slept in them were honored guests, for they were each day honored, borne in their dignity by the care of someone who loved them, these young men growing to middle age and beyond. Their clothes were silently laundered and ironed on the ironing board set up in the kitchen. Even the blue jeans and pajamas were laid out delicately for picking up again, for putting on the body, for filling the imagination with the purpose of the day, these honored men, only half-known, miracles of our incomplete understanding of what we expect in men, that heavy log settled in our eye. For don't they open their arms each day, all color and sound speeding to embrace them? My brother, one among them, rising from his bed, his cradle and beginning, entered an orbit of his own in the company of these brothers, far from their families. In these rooms my brother's many lives were woven, a wrinkled and soon-to-be-ironed cloth, shadows and glints in the folds, a resonance become elemental, almost light, fixed yet fluid, my brother, his brothers, all of a time in a house filled with rooms on Paseo Boulevard.

In the Center, a Person

In 1998, the title of Charlie's evaluation plan had finally changed to "Person Centered Plan," with a full-blown description of my brother as a friend, worker and participant in his community. Various sections titled "Things people say about Charlie. . ." record positive experiences, bringing him into three-dimensional view. Included are statements such as "He's just a real nice guy!" and "He is very independent and likes to do things on his own," and "Hard worker who is awesome at putting labels on boxes." Another section details things Charlie is good at, like "Singing Happy Birthday to his friends and family!" and "Making friends and getting along with housemates." My parents were quick to tell me that most of the credit for Charlie's progress was to the group home where he lived, the Bates Residential Home on Paseo Boulevard in Kansas City's Black community, started by Madeline Bates, a nurse who welcomed children who had lost their parents into her home for care. Charlie lived in four group homes throughout his lifetime, all in Kansas City. The Bates Residential Home was the one he lived in the longest, beginning in 1986 through 2016 when he died. The friends he made there were truly lifelong.

When he first met them, Charlie's five roommates were about his same age, all young men in their late twenties and early thirties, with similar needs as his. Charlie was the only white guy in the group. Most were talkative, a boost for Charlie who needed models for speech and seemed to learn best by imitation. Activities such as dances, bowling, camp and trips to the zoo were supervised by the Bates Home, and often sponsored by our local county. Mrs. Bates' children and grandchildren often participated in activities and care for "the guys," as they were known in the family. Charlie knew Donna Lunn, Mrs. Bates' adopted daughter and the person who took over the group home when Mrs. Bates retired, as well as Donna's children—Josie, Carinne and Stephanie—from the time they were children up through adulthood. This experience, growing up side by side with young men with intellectual disabilities who needed their protection and direction, must not have been easy. When the girls were teenagers, they may have been the targets of mockery for living in the same house as these young men with intellectual disabilities who could not protect them or defend them. The girls were the ones, on Paseo Boulevard, who always loyally stuck up for the guys when sarcastic barbs were hurled their way.

Kansas City, Missouri, in the 1980s and '90s still showed the vestiges of a racist past, harkening back to the violent reconstructionist era after the Civil War. The Paseo Boulevard house was located in the center of the Black community in Kansas City as most Black homebuyers were steered away from middle-class suburbs west of Troost Ave., about a block from Paseo. In 1980, the Census Bureau ranked Kansas City as tenth in the country's most segregated cities. Author G.S. Griffin, in his book *Racism in Kansas City*, cites a study showing that in 1991 Blacks were 2.8 times more likely to be denied a housing loan. In this context, Mrs. Bates began to take care of children in her home on Paseo, starting in the 1970s through the early 2000s when the group home she started moved south to the suburbs. Her daughter Donna told me that starting in the 1970s, from what she recalled, there were many children described as "special needs," as well as older kids like Donna herself, who needed foster care. As the children with intellectual disabilities grew up, they remained in Mrs. Bates' care while she navigated the social services system becoming established for young adults like my brother who had come from a childhood of institutional life or parental abandonment.

Our longest and deepest friendships are often cut from a tweedy swath of material, a mix of age or class or shared experience. Due to Mrs. Bates' and Donna Lunn's efforts, and a new and evolving system of community care, Charlie had a chance to form such friendships with the other guys he lived with in the three-story red-brick house on Paseo Boulevard. One was a man I'll call Al. While Charlie rarely spoke, Al was a master storyteller. When I asked one time what he and Charlie did at the sheltered workshop, he said, "sweep the floor, and drink pop at lunchtime." If you came across the two of them walking down Paseo Boulevard to hang out at the fire station on a hot Kansas City afternoon, you would see two husky men, one bold and purposeful, the other slow and deliberate. Al might greet you with a warm "Hello!" or "Good morning!" and if he thought he knew you, grab your hand in a warm handshake. Al would say quickly, "This is Charlie Anderson, my friend" and Charlie would also extend his hand. Both would project a sense of humor and well-being. Your sense of community would be brightened, meeting them. In contrast to the spontaneous Al, Charlie might seem a little introspective. Although handsome, my brother retained the nervous habits of his youth—fingers dawdling idly, head bent to the side. His shoulders would be rounded and his baggy pants belted high up over his belly. Walking by, he would look past you, forehead furrowed, as if preoccupied. He is a busy person, you would think. From a distance, watching them—Al the amiable, gregarious soul, beside my serious, methodical brother who rarely spoke, I would often wonder about friendship's random beginnings, a kind of love that grows over time and proximity.

The lessons learned by my brother in this group home run by a Black director who hired and supervised the twenty-four-hour staff of direct support professionals, as they are known, would become essential to his social integration. It was important for Charlie to communicate who he was quickly and simply on first meeting, a survival tactic known profoundly by people of color. He was taught, along with his roommates, known as "clients" by the group home direct support professionals, to greet anyone he met with a smile and a handshake. My brother could have been seen as intimidating, but his sincerity in that extended hand was believable and compelling. Many times I saw him dispel someone else's bewilderment on first meeting with that simple gesture. A child who had moved next-door to my parents' home asked me once on meeting him, "Does he speak English?" and then right away added, "He's really got a nice smile!" as she took his hand to shake.

Adopting similar teaching techniques as Eileen used in her classroom, the group home professionals meticulously taught Charlie crucial tactics in case he ever became lost. The method, like the one I witnessed Eileen use with her two young students, was labor-intensive, requiring long patience. It was important that my brother could give his correct name (always stated boldly, "Charles Anderson"), his group home address and phone number if law enforcement found him lost. This was difficult for him. It took Charlie many months to master his new address when the Bates Home moved from Paseo to south of the city. When asked, he would repeat without hesitation the laboriously learned old address and phone number. Teaching him to state his correct age at each new birthday was also a challenge. When asked, "How old are you, Charlie?" he would answer confidently, well into his fifties, that he was "forty-nine." The group home staff let that one go, and kept focused on the more important phone number and new address, which he finally mastered.

In addition to these learning sessions, rewarded with significant applause, treats, or television time, the group home clients were taught fire safety, along with other dangers, such as how to avoid a potential electrical hazard during routine house repair. The direct support professionals kept meticulous logs on every detail of my brother's day: what he ate, his medication dosage, when he went to the bathroom or prepared for bed. They recorded how his teeth were brushed. Each health care or dental visit was documented, entered into a three-ring binder, along with specific directions for at-home care from doctors and dentists.

Out of the group home experience, my brother improved in initiating language, asking for a specific drink, or food he wanted. I remember a time when I came by to pick him up for an outing. I was talking with one of the direct support professionals while he went to get his ball cap, which he liked to wear whenever he went out. I may have been talking too long, because he walked up behind me, cap on his head, ready to go and shouted, "Charlie's a good boy!" I knew immediately that I should stop talking and turn my attention to him. I also realized I needed to stop calling him a "good boy," and change it to "good guy." Charlie was, after all, an adult.

Charlie also showed he understood the good-natured teasing by his roommates. When his pants drooped, and a roommate yelled for him to pull them up, he grinned and giggled. He knew the nicknames of his roommates, their likes and dislikes for foods, all important knowledge to him. Charlie also mastered a series of one-line answers to questions he was asked, a kind of haiku speech that he used with his roommates, co-workers and family. These phrases would flash like comets and disappear just as swiftly. "Nuts and bolts" was the answer he would give my mother when she asked him (many times, perhaps for years) what he did at his sheltered workshop, a strict paper and package kind of place. Once, home from the East Coast, I thought I could prompt him to talk by asking question after question about what he had for lunch, who he drank pop with at work, the name of his group home roommates, etc. He made a few curt tries and then bored by my persistence, gave up, saying, "Shut-up, Cathy." He blinked and cocked his head in triumph. I was thrilled. He was talking to me as if I were one of his friends.

Charlie made steady progress in all aspects of his learning through the 1990s. However, there was one setback. For years, since the time at Fort Custer, Charlie had been on the powerful drug Mellaril. There were at least three periods in which he was taken off the medication to see how he would do. Each time he eventually started to demonstrate severe anxiety and panic, once breaking glass at the workshop and tearing off his shirt. Many of the records from a period in 1991 kept by my mother detail how he had changed without the medication. His facial expression became constantly "worried" she wrote, and he demonstrated labored speech, with less controlled body movements. Additionally, he seemed to ignore the environment around him, dangerously walking straight ahead without looking for traffic. He seemed indifferent to his usual interests, my mother wrote, ignoring colors, foods, fire-engines, pine cones, squirrels, all things that used to capture his attention. The purpose of my mother's statement was to encourage a physician through the Kansas City Regional Center to prescribe Mellaril once again. The statement concludes, "Sadly, the well-intended efforts to have Charles function well without medication have resulted in virtually assigning him an existence we describe as suffering extreme nervous tension and unrelieved stress."

He was put back on a smaller dose of Mellaril but problems increased a few years later when he was admitted as an in-patient at the former Kansas Institute in Olathe, Kansas, about thirty miles from Kansas City. Again, the idea was to transition him from Mellaril, this time to a new medication known as Prozac. My parents expressed extreme skepticism, asserting that with careful maintenance, Charlie was doing well with a minimal dose of Mellaril. The Kansas City Regional Center highly encouraged the examination process to be administered by Dr. Kristopher Kip Wendler, who would treat all the residents of the Bates Residential Home. My parents reluctantly agreed in November of 1993. Within a few weeks it was clear that the hospital stay and switch to Prozac (which my mother always contended was abrupt) had been disastrous for my brother. My mother confronted Dr. Wendler at the consultation and demanded the hospital stop providing services for him. Charlie's behavior had taken another turn for the worse, cancelling any progress he had made in previous years. My parents went to another physician, asking to re-instate his medication. This new physician described Charlie's condition in startling terms in a report from January 1994: "Since beginning Prozac in the fall of 1993, his condition has seemingly deteriorated. Whereas, he used to be capable of grooming himself and pleasantly interactive; in social context, his behavior has been more disheveled, unkempt, and irritable. He noticeably twitches his mouth and his fingers and he found it difficult to keep his legs at rest." This physician recommended a small dosage of Mellaril again, and the use of another drug, Moban, to suppress any involuntary movements that may have been caused by Mellaril. The doctor ends his letter with these words: "I appreciate the opportunity to work with you on this very unfortunate and challenging client."

Within a short time, Charlie did well on the continued small dosage of Mellaril, eventually not needing the Moban. He showed no signs of motor problems such as tardive dyskinesia or vision problems. My mother related the experience at the Kansas Institute, telling me that if I ever had to make a decision about Charlie's medication, not to allow him to be taken off of Mellaril. In January of 1998, I received from my mother a newspaper clipping from the *Kansas City Star* reporting that Dr. Wendler had been indicted by a grand jury for insurance fraud. All the "claims in question were for developmentally disabled adult residents of group homes or residential care facilities in Kanas City," the paper reported. We all felt terribly betrayed on behalf of Charlie and the other group home residents. My mother had been absolutely correct in her distrust of that physician's care. In the year before my brother's death in 2016, Mellaril would still play a detrimental role, but not in the way I had been prepared to monitor or predict.

In our relationship with Charlie, my family and I were concerned for so long about his language deficits that sometimes we couldn't fully appreciate other nonverbal expressions he showed. For instance, while we were happy that he enjoyed running in Special Olympics competitions, earning many medals, we probably didn't understand the primacy of this physical experience in his life. It took time for me to see how my brother's sensual relationship with nature formed his intelligence, the match of his soul to the feeling of his body running in competition, or experiencing a splash of water on his skin. One of the best experiences the group home provided was camp, including supervised swimming. Charlie loved the water, always proclaiming, whenever he saw any small pond, creek, river or lake, "Charlie's water!" Also, for years I never knew how much he liked big machinery. I was taken aback one day, late in our lives together, when he couldn't stop watching a large earthmover in the middle of the road.

It took a long time for me to appreciate another feature of Charlie's conscious life, one that the direct support professionals at the Bates Home recognized immediately: my brother was thinking in pictures, as Temple Grandin so vividly phrased the phenomenon years ago in a book with the same title. She writes, "I translate both spoken and written words into full-color movies, complete with sound. . .When someone speaks to me, his words are instantly translated into pictures." Grandin visualizes pictorial memories and then stores them in her mind like a video library. When a word is used, she scans her library to find a picture matching the word. The word "tree" would never be a general picture of a tree, but a literal one, with particular leaves or needles, depending on the picture Grandin had filed of a tree she once saw.

My brother had demonstrated Grandin's kind of thinking when he was a little boy and stuck the catalog picture of electric lights on the fuse box. Charlie's language was always noun-heavy and most responsive to concrete objects and their representation. As he grew older, he responded well to children's picture books, and delighted in games on his iPad that challenged him to identify pictures with words. This was a child's teaching game, but the seriousness with which he grabbed the iPad and sat down to focus, as if it were his *job*, was an indication of the primacy of the visual in his thinking. As much as we tried to teach him letters on a computer keyboard, he declined interest, but the pictures on the iPad could fascinate him for hours. At the sheltered workshop, Charlie did his best performing various tasks by following visual cues and his meticulous fine-motor skills were highly valued. He was known to be proficient in precisely placing labels on boxes, and called on more than once, we were proud to learn, for special projects to be completed on deadline.

Charlie was doing so well, much better than anyone would have predicted when he was a child, yet the intense myth of his birth and my mother's advice to forgo motherhood were deeply embedded in me. As I entered my mid-thirties, I was afraid, perhaps unnecessarily, that having a child with intellectual disabilities would be beyond my capabilities. I had long decided that if I was not in a relationship by the time I was thirty-five, I wouldn't risk becoming pregnant. Soon I was that age and single. This decision, one both my parents, of course, understood, still made me feel like a salmon swimming upstream against the cultural current. In my journal I captured the feeling then as one of sorrow, "a permanent blue in the soul." One day, looking for a present for Charlie in the preschool aisle of a toy store, I knew I would never shop for a child of my own. I traced this sorrow, voicing again the negativity I had absorbed, back to my brother's difficult birth: "my brother born blue, blue wings over a backyard." I felt the heavy weight of renunciation in my life: "I will be the still woman, the one who adds no sorrow to the world." Thankfully, this flash of sensitive self-regard didn't last. Did I truly believe someone like my brother contributed to the world's sorrow? No. My brother, and those like him, through their sensitivity and efforts to belong in a challenging culture, communicated far more wisdom than many neurotypical people.

Another surprise was the rainy day I watched Charlie bowl. Everyone knew he was quite good at it, scoring many strikes for the group home team. When I watched him in that March championship competition, I noticed that he spent the time waiting for his turn by watching the crowd, not the game, his eyes scanning the audience. I waved at him and then moved around the audience to get a better view. When it was his turn to bowl, he had to be tapped on the shoulder and told to get his ball. He took long strides up to the lane with laconic ease that could have been self-assurance. He then closed one eye and released the ball. He didn't stay to watch the ball make its jagged ramble down the alley to triumphantly strike all the pins. He didn't raise his arms in the air like a winner. He didn't beam a smile. He didn't have to because he had no doubt at all about his ability to strike down the pins. Instead, Charlie took an about-face from the bowling lane to wide-pan his team and the audience, now applauding and shouting his name.

The Bates Residential Home created a community, a social dynamic that emerged from close relationships, one my family and I never expected to witness. We were very grateful. My brother, so enamored of my mother's dinners and all varieties of food, soon found a way to express his feeling of community by helping in the kitchen at mealtimes. He cleared the table after everyone finished, carrying out this duty at every table he graced, even helping the restaurant server when we would take him out to eat. He also helped to carry groceries in, putting everything away where it belonged, just as he did when he was a kid. He was careful about his belongings, always returning his sunglasses to the same dresser drawer. He took care of his clothes, each morning selecting them for work carefully, preferring blue shirts with jeans. He never left a towel on the floor, folding it and hanging it on the rack after a shower, his last act before going to bed. Through these objects and their care, he knew he belonged in this community, a beloved one, a caring one.

All relationships compel us to apply the craft of an artist: to use color and sound, gesture, light, and silence. A relationship with someone like my brother is a similar kind of journey, keeping in mind we will never fully comprehend how the other person thinks. After visiting home to see Charlie and my family one spring, I spent a few weeks in a cabin by a meadow edging the foothills of Mount Monadnock in New Hampshire. In the evening, I settled down in a lawn chair as the high call and response notes of the wood thrushes began echoing through the trees. I lay back and listened, truly listened, for more than half an hour—each song folded into the next, riff on riff, light trills floating through the firs until the sun fell. Then silence. Like my brother's halting, spiraling echoes, I thought, these half-answered words and staccato utterances. In the mountain's shadow I realized that I needed nothing more. If I could accept these early evening bird calls for what they were—sounds beyond my understanding—I could accept my brother in all of the expressive range he possessed, whether it be silent, voiced, or kinetic.

LAKE OF WORDS

Many of us believe language makes us whole. We are not who we think we are until we can speak our mind, as the expression goes. We have not arrived at a place or a country, or even a phase in life until we can somehow put our feelings about it into words. My brother Charlie may not have felt exactly like that, I've come to realize. Yet my experience with him often left me wondering what it must feel like *not* to be in full mastery of a language and still have to speak it out of necessity. How much of a language do we need to belong to a culture, a community, or a country?

On a plane to Cuba one July when I was twenty-seven, I found myself interpreting for an older gentleman next to me who didn't understand the flight attendant. I'd had two semesters in college of Spanish, a language I studied alongside French and German, and although I felt moderately confident reading these languages, I never mastered speaking them. The man was grateful for my tourist Spanish and immediately began to flirt, which I deflected, totally surprised again by what came out of my mouth. This experience, even before landing, gave me the confidence to stumble through tours of a Cuban farm cooperative and a dental clinic, a night meeting with the neighborhood central committee, and numerous encounters with Cubans where my slow, stilted questions were met with infinite patience.

The purpose of our trip was educational. I was interested in the presence of a Communist country within our own hemisphere, and in the economic inequities of Latin countries caused, in part, by U.S. domination. In Cuba, I was the awkward North American speaking Spanish, one of the most mellifluous tongues of the world. Even though I could bounce back to the safety of my English-speaking companions, I loved sinking into the oblivion of sounds I could only partially comprehend on the streets of Havana and Cienfuegos. I could afford the aesthetic experience. I was on vacation. I didn't have to survive by how I spoke to find a job or a place to live, unlike the thousands of immigrants and refugees who have made the United States their home. But it was a vacation that taught me the precarious status of a developing country, less than one hundred miles off the U.S. coast. An economic blockade over decades initiated by the U.S. meant food shortages and peeling paint, jerry-rigged generators and few luxuries. Yet side by side were astounding riffs of music and the ever-present poetry of Jose Martí. A country like Cuba challenged me because it demanded I pay attention not only to what I perceived but how I was perceived, as white, as North American. That was one lesson I took home to Boston where I lived.

A few years later I put my intermediate Spanish to use by working with adult students learning English. Every morning through fall, winter and spring of 1985 and 1986, I met with groups of adults, mostly women from Puerto Rico, the Dominican Republic, Cape Verde and Haiti, and mostly mothers who were poor and lived in Boston's Roxbury and Dorchester neighborhoods. We gathered in an old classroom that was once Boston College High School where generations of working-class kids learned calculus and catechism inside its nineteenth-century brick structure centered in the heart of the South End, before the area became gentrified. The school was not far from the Cathedral of the Holy Cross and right across the street from Boston City Hospital, known as the inspiration for the hit television series *St. Elsewhere*. When I described this job to my parents, they told me how they watched the show's opening scene to see the neighborhood where I worked, drawing close to the screen to follow the slender Orange line train as it curved along the old elevated tracks above Washington Street, past the compact hospital and tall brownstones shelved between the narrow streets.

A fine layer of dust covered everything in the cavernous classroom, from the boxes of old math books by the door to the rows of tiny, hobbled desks etched with ink stains. Yellow linoleum, pocked and bumpy, covered the tilted floors. If you dropped a pencil, it rolled across the room, lost to dust balls nested under a pile of broken chairs. The train rattled the windows every fifteen minutes or so, interrupting our class. No one minded any of this and I didn't either. The adult women I met that first day of class arrived as loud and passionate students, eager to make new friends and start their schooling, and perhaps their lives, all over again. They had not finished high school, and this was their chance to catch up. Many were bilingual, coming to the United States from Puerto Rico, perhaps, at a young age, and often traveling back and forth for years between Boston and the island. A few women told me that their fathers had pulled them out of school when they turned twelve, believing they would meet boys there and become pregnant. Another woman, a bit older than the others, told me when she started high school in Boston after arriving from Puerto Rico, a counselor advised her to drop out because she didn't know enough English. Some students told me they had to give up their chance for an education because their families had no money, or a mother was ill and the family needed a daughter at home to cook and do laundry.

Entering class that first day, many in our class were dressed in their very best—bright dresses with high heels and jewelry. They carried dictionaries and mock-leather briefcases. How was I to live up to their expectations? I followed their lead in the next few weeks and dressed up too. I couldn't wait to channel their vibrant energy into vivid prose. In addition to the basics, I intended to teach the tools of the writing trade, from the intricate verbs and contradictory spelling of the English language to dense, compelling paragraphs. That was my hope at least. I would be teaching four classes throughout the day, instructing a range of people—those who spoke English fluently but never learned to write to those who'd only learned English by ear.

After four years, I had just left a job teaching English literature and composition in a Catholic private secondary school in Newton, an upper end suburb of Boston. Even though initially I loved teaching high school-age girls, the social-economic class collisions were difficult to handle. At one point, I almost lost my job when I told someone I'd spent some time in Cuba over the summer. I found this job through a friend, Sister Carlota Duarte, a photographer who had documented the lives of South Enders. She connected me to Carmelo Iglesias, the Puerto Rican tenants' rights activist who had started a program for indigent women receiving what was known then as Aid to Families with Dependent Children. In Massachusetts, recipients had to attend classes to maintain their allotment. Carmelo realized the need for remedial classes in English, writing, math, and computer skills and created the program called Casa del Sol (House of the Sun). In my interview, I convinced him of my knack for explaining complex grammar and my interest in the lives of poor women from developing countries now living in Boston. I had never worked in low-income communities before but he still took a chance on me.

The textbooks stored in the back of the room were all from the 1950s and '60s, not much use. The ancient chalkboard resisted my sprawling handwriting, which was just as well. I bought magic markers and wrote on a big tablet, each day tearing off the lake of words we'd assembled in class: names for items in a kitchen, irregular verbs, ways to say hello, parts of the body, clothes worn in winter, clothes in summer. In one of the dusty boxes, I found some blue mimeographed grammar exercises and carefully rationed those as long as I could. Casa del Sol had an irritable copy machine, usually delivering copies so powdery, the words blew away with one flick of the wrist. I wrote government agencies to collect free pamphlets everyone could use as reading material, and so for a few weeks we all learned about car insurance fraud (even though no one had a car, including me), how to discern choices of meat, how to hire a lawyer, or buy a house.

It was obvious that none of this material was useful to the women in our class who had more dire concerns, such as the threat of eviction, or their children becoming swept up in gangs. I ran across a booklet published by an anti-poverty group that offered instructions with diagrams showing how to make a warm jacket by duct-taping layers of discarded newspapers. How could I pass on this grim information, so without hope, to these students? Two of them, newly arrived from Haiti, and in shock from the New England cold, came to class wearing every item of clothing they owned, one flowery cotton dress on top of the other. Stories the women brought with them each morning to share, their own stories of triumph, loss, abuse, and love were far more intriguing than car insurance. When I asked them to write down their stories, suddenly the class gained momentum. I based our grammar lessons on these events of the day, making a column for "good news" and "bad news." This worked. I could throw out the meat pamphlets, the blue mimeographed pages and the odd books by well-intentioned realists.

One day I was explaining "I wish I could" phrasing, those conditional constructions that spark a speaker's dreams or force a coming to terms with a missed chance. To get things going I asked, "What do you wish you could do?" and a woman answered, "I wish I could see the sunset." In my rush to provide solutions, one of many mistakes I would make, I turned to the class and said, "Where could we go to see the sunset?" I was looking for the answer already in my head: take the subway to the beach at Savin Hill in Dorchester, or go north to Revere. All my solutions involved packing up the kids and planning a trip away from the neighborhood. The class was silent. Finally, someone else said, "You don't understand. In my country, you could look out the door every evening and watch the sun set over the ocean. It is very important and I miss it so much."

It has always been the privilege of whiteness to walk away, to forget what was just witnessed in the lives of people of color. I felt a similar pang when I thought about the years Charlie was institutionalized, when I enjoyed the privilege of a so-called normal life. After teaching at Casa del Sol for two years, I spent another three years working more intensely with a literacy movement begun in Dorchester, the heart of the Latino community of Boston at the time. The program there was called Mujeres Unidas en Acción (Women United in Action), primarily run by Latinas, and committed to providing literacy classes founded on the theories of Paulo Freire, the Brazilian educator. According to Freire, a teacher was not a banker of knowledge but a facilitator, and the learning process was a two-way street, with the teacher placed often in the role as student, conveying respect and interest in the student's life outside the classroom.

This educational approach resembled the care I had witnessed in Eileen's class, and in the care Charlie was receiving at the Bates Residential Home—an enormous respect for the central dignity of the person. Applied to language learning, the approach also assumed language was not just an exchange of words, but a three-dimensional experience going beyond gestures and facial expression, demanding attention to culture, personal history, geography and economics. The teachers encouraged creative problem solving by inviting the experiences of new English speakers in identifying their own solutions for change in the community. How they did this was on the surface very simple, yet yielded intense language learning. In summary, which doesn't do the method justice, a teacher would select a photograph of a dramatic moment that illustrates a problem: A family evicted from their apartment, for example. The teacher would then ask questions to build vocabulary and perhaps reinforce pronunciation: "Who is in the picture? What are the people doing? What is their problem?" These questions would be compelling to the student, not simply rote practice. Students would respond with their own ideas and their own experience. The approach, still used today in basic literacy classes, taps into the ancient art of storytelling as a path to gaining wisdom and control in life and community. It creates positive energy because it actively involves students.

At that time I was meeting passionate activists supporting rights to education, healthcare, housing and drug treatment who were able to put their ideas into immediate action at the local level. One activist, Mel King, had led a tent city of protesters camped for months in Boston's South End, in opposition to a shiny new development in Copley Square, and in favor of housing for low-income residents. He was a tall, bearded Black man with a stentorian voice and gentle manner. At one of our graduations at Casa del Sol, King spoke of everyone's right, as a participating member of a community, to ownership of what he called the *land*. King defined land in the broadest terms. It meant all things necessary for a human being to live with dignity: a home, a job, an education. These essentials were what he and the group of activists inhabiting tent city were fighting for in those heady days of Boston urban redevelopment when forgotten areas of the city were sold for a high price. To possess those essentials meant a person, whatever language they spoke, whatever country they came from, belonged to a community. The graduates of our program, King said, now possessed this land. When I heard him speak, I realized that for Charlie, back in Kansas City, a home, a job, and a community were within reach in ways my family never would have thought possible. This was now my brother's land, too. He was becoming someone who belonged, no longer an outsider.

V
MY BROTHER'S TABLE

House Empty Now

Before my mother died in August of 1999, she gave us the words we needed to talk about her death with my brother Charlie. Tell him this, she said: "Mother loved Charlie very much, but Mother got sick and couldn't come home again." She phrased it in the idiosyncratic grammar my family used when speaking with him—direct, to the point, and without personal pronouns like *you* or *she* because Charlie didn't use these words.

Our mother also didn't speak the word *death* when telling us what to tell my brother and she didn't raise the expectation that we take over his daily care. She did expect me to become my brother's legal guardian once my father, who survived her, passed away. And she expressed a hope that Charlie's life would continue without change at the Bates Residential Home and the sheltered workshop. Over the years I tried, with effort, to fulfill that promise. I am the eldest child and only daughter in the family, my arms permanently open to catch whatever falls.

Mom had a lilting Southern cadence to her speech, given to generous descriptions and well-turned metaphors. She loved the beauty of the human voice, as expressive vehicle or musical instrument. This love led her to assist people from all walks of life, especially in her early years in Detroit—children born with cleft palates, wounded war veterans, refugees new to the English language. The shape of the tongue reaching for the letter "r" or the stop of breath required for the sound of "d" at the end of a word were movements whose perfection she knew instinctively, the way a dancer knows the forms of the bolero or the saraband. I've always thought that one of the central ironies of my mother's life was to give birth to a child who needed her full professional expertise to learn how to talk. She certainly rose to the challenge, as difficult as it was. Both Charlie and I learned our love for the sensual beauty of nature from her, our mother born in the peninsular state of Florida with its palms and coasts, and Charlie and I born on another peninsula to the north, known for its pines and lakes. Even though we conflicted so many times, my mother and I sustained a deep connection. I was with her in her last days. I remember another thing she said when Charlie came to visit, "It all worked out. I had no idea it would."

Our mother was a cigarette smoker for almost forty-five years. She had tried to quit several times and succeeded months before we heard the dispiriting news of her terminal lung cancer. She claimed that nicotine took the edge off her nerves, and during my childhood both parents filled ashtrays throughout the day, the house dense with smoky dust motes. In January of 1999 when I flew from my home to be with her in Kansas City the night she was diagnosed, she told me, "Don't feel sorry for me. I loved smoking." It started as a form of rebellion in the conservative south of the 1940s. With her girlfriends in tow, my mother used to drive down Tampa's Bayshore Boulevard with four or five cigarettes hanging from her mouth, a stunt to razz the more sedate onlookers. Toward the end, she breathed with the assistance of a portable oxygen canister, her voice still melodious between outbursts of coughing.

The evening of our mother's wake, Bill and I picked up Charlie from the group home where he waited for us, holding his good clothes on a hanger. Back at the house on W. 63rd St., the one Charlie knew as his family home, we helped him put on his shirt and suit jacket, we clipped a few fingernails, and buzzed his chin with the electric razor, just as our mother would have done on Sunday mornings before church. A funeral home was not a church, but its close resemblance would make it easier for him to understand what was going on, Bill and I reassured each other. There would be people he knew, candles, hand-shaking, flowers. Charlie liked to follow rituals, to imitate what others were doing. But would he realize that his mother had just died? He had never been to a funeral before. We didn't know if Mom would be laid out in an open casket because our father, who had made the arrangements, didn't remember. This could be a problem, Bill and I realized. On the way to the funeral home, we repeated as carefully as we could the words of farewell our mother had told us to tell him. He frowned, eyeing the road ahead as we drove. Entering the visitation area of the funeral home Bill and I soon saw the open casket, and our mother laid out in a blue Swiss-dot dress. In silence, we each walked up to her and gave our parting words. When it was Charlie's turn to say good-bye, he stood over the casket, looked down at his mother's face, and then raised his hand toward her, speaking in a loud voice, "Good-bye Mummer, good-bye Mama, good-bye Doris Anderson." Finished, he turned to join the rest of us who were watching, in awe.

♪❃♡❃♩

Through the one large window of my studio apartment in Cambridge, Massachusetts, I watched light settle as the red brick of the building reflected a glowing amber and a sliver of sky turned claret blue. The winter solstice, the shortest day of that memorable year of 2001, was coming to a close. I watched a few minutes longer as this transition took place, knowing it would be my last glance out this window, my 600-square-foot studio completely empty of furniture and possessions after twenty-two years. The next day I was leaving permanently for my family home in Kansas City, Missouri. I would spend my final night in Cambridge not here, but at a friend's house. Everyone in our apartment building had been served eviction notices months before as the building was changing to condominiums. In late December of 2001, I was single, forty-seven years old, had a second book of poems published and a job I loved in healthcare advocacy. Yet I was leaving this life behind for my father's house in the middle of the Midwest. Because of lingering laryngitis, I had no voice, but I also had no words at that time to explain the pull I felt in going back to a place I had left twenty-five years ago, never expecting to return. My friends were graciously silent in their questioning and loyally supportive, but I know I left them wondering what the hell I was doing.

I was returning for a number of reasons—my limited housing choices, my widowed father's diminishing health, and most importantly, a chance to connect with my brother Charlie who needed me, his best friend in the world, since our mother had died two years ago. I had no illusions about replacing our mother, but only knew I had to try to be a good sister now that we both had entered middle age. How else could I do this without moving to where he lived? Charlie and I had lived apart, in separate cities, since I was ten years old and he was seven. He didn't read or write, so we had no written correspondence. He didn't like telephones, barely speaking a quick "Hi Cahtee, bye Cahtee" whenever I called him.

Departures and arrivals, arrivals and departures. Whenever I flew home from the East Coast to Kansas City, I would tell Charlie about the big plane I took, the high-up clouds and sky I saw from the window. He listened, watching my mouth as I spoke the words, following my hands as I gestured upward. Our family history is a story of arrivals and departures and Charlie lived no different a life. My brother Bill had promised to pick me up at the airport when I landed in Kansas City with my laptop, and six bags of luggage containing all my clothes and some personal items. The connecting flight from Chicago that had passed over the snow-crusted, circular fields of Iowa and into the rolling brown of Missouri reminded me of train trips I had taken when I was younger from Chicago to Missouri, when the land widened and everyone's chatter grew louder and louder on the approach to Union Station in Kansas City. Those long trips home I used to take helped me to process my family and so much of what we had experienced when Charlie and I were children. Now I would be home again, trying to understand a new range of circumstances. The flight was on time in the late afternoon, another shortened day ending in a gold, pearly hue. I was at the back, deplaning slowly, entering the gate and looking for my brother Bill. I waved when I saw Bill's face and then my dad's and then I saw someone I hadn't expected, a tall man about ready to break into laughter as he towered over the people gathered at the receiving area—Charlie. Beaming a brilliant smile, he called out "Cahtee!" I waved even harder. He kept smiling and smiling. I knew at that moment I would never turn back.

Within a year and a half after moving back to Kansas City, I had moved in with my boyfriend Neil Bull, who lived near my father. Within three years, on a lark, we decided to get married. We did it as an excuse to have a party for all our friends and announce our love for each other, but also because we knew we were no longer young (Neil was fourteen years older than I) and our days would reach an end point. We had a joyous wedding in our backyard garden that May, with Charlie in attendance, shouting "Say Cheese!" whenever a camera was pointed our way. At the following Thanksgiving, when Charlie was setting the table, stating each person's name as he put down a plate, we saw him hovering over Neil's place, speaking in a low-pitched voice. Neil said to me, "I think he just called me Neil Anderson." I then pointed to Neil and asked Charlie who this was. He swiftly answered "NeilAnderson!" blending my husband's given name with our family surname, thus establishing Neil's role, forever, in the family circle.

When I met Neil, he had just retired as a professor of sociology at the University of Missouri/Kansas City. A seasoned observer of people, he had spent part of his career analyzing policies on rural health care, then poking around small Missouri towns assisting agencies who provided services to senior citizens. Born outside of Blackpool, England, and raised all over the United Kingdom in the 1940s and 1950s, he knew postwar scarcity firsthand. This experience helped him understand why seniors often refused assistance even when they desperately needed it. When I talked with Neil, I understood my father's resistance to my help more clearly. With careful planning, the future of my father's care became not so frightening. All of these attributes certainly enhanced my esteem for Neil but what convinced me that we could have a lot of fun together was the research concentration of his early career in sociology: leisure. My mate was a scholar of the relaxed life, a bona fide expert! Now, in retirement, he could spend well-deserved time in the field, reporting new insights and I could join him whenever I could get away. The secret to the life of leisure, I learned from Neil, was getting all the work you hated out of the way early in the day. Then relax. Listen to music. Go for a walk. Go out for Chinese food. Another secret was to clean as little as possible, relying on time-saving products. With that advice, I stopped vacuuming my father's four-bedroom house and stopped making meals for him in advance, relying on frozen dinners. I realized he mainly didn't care about a clean house or great meals, neither of which I was good at providing. My father simply wanted me to hang out and talk with him.

Charlie loved to listen to Neil's clipped Midlands accent, especially when he pronounced the word "been" as "bean," or sped up the end of his sentences, in contrast to the long-drawn-out vowels of the Kansas City region. Charlie would follow Neil's mouth as he talked, often smiling or breaking up into laughter. Neil was there to witness the first time I saw Charlie stand up and speak in public. We had taken him to our local library to hear a concert and lecture by a folksinger who was introducing Missouri River tunes from the French fur trading era. The music was gentle yet lively, and I could tell my brother enjoyed it. At the end, the musician talked a bit about the origin of the songs and asked if there were any questions. Charlie, who rarely initiated conversation in private, jumped out of his seat and began to speak words that were hard to understand but had the intonation of a person asking information. The speaker graciously thanked Charlie. Both Neil and I were astounded. Later, I learned from his sheltered workshop supervisor that often he would stand up and ask a question during a work informational presentation. I had no idea.

Charlie was still game for the old standby jokes we exchanged when our mother was alive. I'd take him to the garden Neil tended in the backyard, pick up a tomato, show it to him and call it a "blue tomato." Just as I thought, he would quickly correct me, "No! Tomato red!" insisting with all the power of his belief, that however right I was about so many complicated things, about this very important item, I was absolutely wrong. To further encourage Charlie to speak I suggested we try to use social modeling, also called social learning. Social modeling requires two people to interact with the person receiving the training. It differs from operant conditioning because the emphasis is on a relationship with the person being encouraged to speak, another person responding, and the person asking questions. It is also rooted in observation and imitation, natural ways most people learn. I first read about it in Temple Grandin's *Animals in Translation* where Grandin relates how Dr. Irene Pepperberg taught her parrot, the loquacious Alex, to speak through social modeling. The key to Dr. Pepperberg's social modeling success was that instead of teaching Alex directly, she taught another person while Alex watched, creating a rivalry. Alex became motivated to compete for Dr. Pepperberg's attention, and by watching his rival, learned the new word. This technique sounded just novel enough to help Charlie speak more spontaneously. My expectations were low: no dramatic self-revelation, no stand-up comedy or childhood jokes pouring forth. I simply wanted to expand his limited repertoire of words.

In a conversation with Charlie, I included Neil, Charlie's friendly companion, if not rival. To start off, I asked NeilAnderson what he liked to eat. "I like hamburgers," he responded, of course, and before the words were barely out of his mouth, Charlie jumped in to say, "Charlie like hamburger." Then I asked Neil to count to ten. Almost on cue, Charlie started to count. After that, we tried social modeling conversations as a way to describe new experiences or lighten instructions on hygiene and safety. For example, I handed both Neil and Charlie a Kleenex and then turned to Neil: "Neil, do you have a Kleenex?" Neil: "Yes, I do. It's in my pocket." Charlie jumped in right away, mimicking Neil: "Charlie, Kleenex, pocket." He put the Kleenex in his pocket and tapped the top of my hand to make sure I'd noticed what he did! Previously, when one of us would ask him a question directly, he would respond infrequently or lethargically. This was the first time my brother had touched me to get my attention.

At this time, my father's health problems were making it impossible for him to live alone without help. I was also afraid dementia was slowly setting in. I had already started to take over doing his bills. Reluctantly, I took my father to live at Armour Home, an assisted living center and nursing home we had checked out together, only a few miles away. It was a Saturday morning in April, and the redbud tree he loved to view from his kitchen window was in full bloom. A day earlier we had packed a few of his things in a suitcase and talked about what kind of room he would have, where he would eat dinner, how often I would come to visit. My father showed me the small army green rucksack he had owned since his discharge from the infantry. I realized that he did not understand this move was permanent. In this bag he had packed the items he wanted to take to the nursing home: a comb, his checkbook, eyeglasses case and a pair of pliers he used to open jars and bottles. My father had rheumatoid arthritis, his hands curved into claws that grasped clumsily at doorknobs and chairs. When he had been a newspaper reporter his hands once banged on an Underwood manual at sixty words per minute, typing through the Civil Rights movement, the Vietnam War and the invasion of Czechoslovakia. Now they were almost nonfunctional.

The story of a parent's decline is the sound of ripping cloth and quiet tears, of choked-back anger and sighs of relief. My father lasted one week in the assisted living center of Armour Home before he had to be moved to the home's nursing unit. Within that time, I needed more money to pay for his care and began the process to sell the family house, the one Charlie knew as home. Everything in the four-bedroom house would have to go, all the papers sifted, all the pots and pans boxed, all the beds unframed, the rugs rolled up. One morning I began with the kitchen, taking down the stainless-steel frying pan whose handle my mother had cleverly mended by winding ordinary cotton string around and around, then coating it with Elmer's glue to seal the grip. Next were the blue cow-shaped cream pitcher, the wooden spice rack, the line of flour sack-shaped canisters, the roasting pan, the nested mixing bowls, the plastic cup measures, all packed in large boxes.

Only five months after his move to the Armour Home, my father died. I was with him at the time, late at night in his room. I had now witnessed both my parents' deaths.

At my home after the funeral, my brother Bill and I marveled at the different approaches to death our parents had taken. Our father at first resisted going gentle into that good night, while our mother accepted her diagnosis of terminal cancer from the beginning with no fear. Both showed gratitude and respect for the medical and nursing staff trusted to care for them, asking about their lives and sharing jokes. We both were thankful for these lessons in the acceptance of death. After our mother died, our father had lived for another six years with multiple illnesses. He had experienced so many brushes with death, we concluded, he couldn't stop fighting, even when the odds were stacked against him. The list of near misses we knew about included five major battles as an infantryman, a plane crashing right beside his car as he traveled the expressway home one morning after working midnights, a gasoline truck exploding in front of him on that same Detroit expressway, and a metal projectile hitting his car windshield in Kansas City. He was eighty-one when he died.

That afternoon Bill and I decided to take Charlie for a last look at the old house before it would be sold and out of our lives forever. The late September air was brisk, with leaves scattered by strong winds riding down from the Rockies. The house was a quick stride from my home with Neil. Charlie gained speed as we approached. We let him walk ahead to the back steps, the path he knew so well. At the door, I turned the key and said to both my brothers, "The house is empty now." When the door opened, Charlie bolted past us through the kitchen, opening closets, cupboards, announcing aloud over and over, "House. Empty. Now. House. Empty." To Charlie, losing the house meant the same thing as losing his father and mother. His words became softer and softer as he wound through the other rooms, until his voice became no more than a whisper to himself, "house empty now."

A sheer surprise, his quiet echo. For a few more minutes Charlie, Bill and I stood together with our own thoughts in that empty house. Then we left, locked the door, and trudged through the afternoon's fallen leaves.

FAITHFUL TO THE WORD

I donated those pots, pans, cups and saucers from my mother's kitchen to Jewish Vocational Service (JVS) in Kansas City, the largest refugee resettlement agency in the city, where I worked. The refugees JVS serves come primarily from the African continent, the Middle East, and the countries of Asia. At the time of my father's transition to the nursing home, a group of Somali Bantu families had just arrived. Most had been living in an impoverished and dangerous refugee camp in northern Kenya for over a decade. Mothers, grandmothers, children, fathers and grandfathers landed at Kansas City International Airport with perhaps one bag of personal items. They usually arrived in the middle of the night as they had many flight changes before reaching Kansas City. They were met by JVS staff who took them to a pre-arranged apartment, and made sure they had a dinner of traditional Somali food before they went to bed for the first time in the U.S. Their next number of days would be filled with bureaucratic necessities: applying for a Social Security number and enrolling kids in school. They would need to visit a local clinic for a federally required health exam and any necessary health treatment.

The first months were a dizzy entry for these new refugees, resembling Charlie's when he was released from the institution—a rapid acquisition of new words in English for foods, sounds and objects never seen before. Children had to start school, and parents had to get jobs as the federal funds they received ended after ninety days. In a new country, they had to learn at lightning speed all about U.S. currency, traffic, city buses, as well as stoves and refrigerators, microwaves and cell phones. They needed warm clothes to wear to work and school. To cook for their families, they needed my mother's plates and cups, her pots and dishes, including that mended frying pan. Some of them could converse in Somali with other Somalis who had moved to Kansas City years before, but most spoke Maay Maay, a Bantu language. An English-as-a-Second-Language cooking class was designed for them by a teacher whose rigor and humor reminded me of Mr. Stark in my eleventh-grade biology class. The teacher would hold my mother's wooden spoon in the air, the way Mr. Stark would show us a pipette, and after the interpreter stated the name of the spoon in Maay Maay, the teacher stated the name in English, requiring each Somali woman to repeat after her. They were learning

English in the quickest, most practical way, by adapting Somali recipes to the foods found in Kansas City stores.

I had started working at JVS a few years before, heading a program charged with training new interpreters from refugee communities who would then be paid to provide interpreting services across the city. The Somali women in the cooking class knew the newspaper-wrapped items I delivered in rattling cardboard boxes came from my mother's kitchen. They knew my mother had been a teacher who was no longer alive. After class one of the Somali interpreters told me that often the women lingered in the training kitchen, enjoying each other's company. Young and old, the women would lean back, sip coffee from my mother's tea cups, and think of her, a woman and mother like them. It was such a kind thought to share with me.

My experience with the range of Charlie's communication styles was one of the best preparations I could have had for this job, which involved over two dozen languages spoken by the refugees and immigrants who had resettled in our region over the course of about thirty years. They included multiple Burmese languages, as well as Pashto and Dari, spoken by new Afghan arrivals, and the many languages of Africa such as Kinyarwanda, Swahili, or Somali. After witnessing for years my brother's attempts to communicate, to be present in the world where he could be seen and understood, I knew language was more than a linguistic transaction. It requires the use of multiple actions—gestures, facial expression, positioning, voice register and intonation on the part of both the listener and the speaker. One thing I picked up right away was the importance of the English speaker (doctor or social worker) to convey their willingness to help the non-English speaker become visible and heard, right there, in the exam room or office. They do this by working closely with an interpreter who keeps in the background, facilitating communication. In spoken language interpreting, the interpreter often sits or stands behind the non-English speaker so that the focus is on the relationship between the patient (or client) and the provider. The interpreter is a neutral party in the session, and literally, a voice, a conduit. Interpreters for the deaf remain less in the background primarily so their signing can be seen. Both professionals work to be sure the non-English speaker's (or deaf client's) words are understood, and that the client also understands the information communicated in English.

Because an interpreter works behind the scenes, the experience is a bit unnatural. It is much more formal than a typical conversation. Constant training is necessary, almost as if a person were training for the theater, but not quite as the interpreter always works within the realm of reality. For example, one young man, a Swahili and Kinyarwanda speaker, with mastery in English, came to my office once announcing he didn't know why he was here that day, but he would find out. He was an evangelist, he told me. His job was to advocate for people in his community. That was his first priority. Interpreting, I would tell him, requires control of that urge to advocate. He would soon learn how to become a neutral voice, a conduit of information between two people who speak different languages. In this role as a skilled interpreter he would be a significant help to his community.

Charlie's struggles to be seen and understood laid the foundation for much of my passion to understand not only how communication takes place, but how to protect the essential *right* of a non-English speaker to an interpreter when conducting the serious business of health care, social services, legal matters and education. It's common sense that only a trained interpreter, one who knows both English and the target language, would be able to facilitate this communication. Finding someone with this talent is difficult. In assessing an interpreter's ability to interpret, I've often tried to evaluate, among many things, an interpreter's understanding of what they *don't know*, essential for accurate communication. To determine this, I've used a number of language proficiency screens, situational scenarios and other methods. I always reinforced the interpreter's code of ethics with its emphasis on confidentiality and boundaries.

Very often the need for accurate interpreting has not been taken seriously, rendering non-English speakers invisible. I first saw this time and time again while working in the Latino community of Boston in the 1980s. I would learn even more about the complexities of facilitating communication between languages in the early 1990s when I worked for three years in Boston's Chinatown as the English editor of *Sampan*, a bilingual community newspaper published by the Asian American Civic Association. In collaboration with the Chinese editor, I worked to put out a biweekly that reached thousands all over New England in English and Mandarin Chinese. We each covered similar events, but in our own languages, and not translated. The Chinese editor and I worked with more clarity and nuance writing our separate articles, striving to highlight the voices of those who were advocating on behalf of a wide Asian community, including second-generation immigrants, as well as new Vietnamese residents within the small geographic circumference of Boston's original South Cove.

The need in Chinatown for skilled interpreters was the theme of a talk one day in 1991 by Caroline Chang, the Regional Manager for the Office for Civil Rights for the U.S. Department of Health and Human Services. Chang's focus was the Civil Rights Act of 1964 and especially how the law impacted health care. I intended to write an article for *Sampan* on this problem, aware of many residents who had been turned away by the nearby acute care hospital, Tufts New England Medical Center, because the hospital had no available Chinese or Vietnamese interpreters. Often this happened in the middle of the night when a non-English speaker came into the emergency room. They were told to go to Boston City Hospital, miles away. Or they had to receive care in English, a language they didn't understand. Chang informed us that this act, our country's main anti-discrimination law, contains a protection for people who don't speak English. Title VI of the law "prohibits discrimination on the basis of race, color, or national origin in any program or activity that receives Federal funds or other Federal financial assistance." Institutions that receive federal funds—schools, social service agencies and hospitals, among others—are required to provide equal access to services, meaning access to skilled interpreting, free of charge. Any of the institution's forms and documents used by the public need to be translated into languages of the catchment population. The law was clear, but the implementation of it uneven. Certainly, the Tufts New England Medical Center did not follow this law when they turned away Vietnamese- and Chinese-speaking patients who needed care.

I could picture the crux of the problem instantly. Those stories of patients at a loss to understand what was causing their illness reminded me of times when my family had no idea what was wrong with Charlie because in a sense, *we didn't speak his language.* Watching my parents' struggles with Charlie and the medical system fueled my intention to showcase the critical importance of expert interpretation as a means of quality care. Equity doesn't exist unless a person can understand their diagnosis, their prescription, their legal sentence, their child's report card. Chang answered questions for the article I was writing with care. She was a noted leader who had grown up on Chinatown's Hudson Ave. Her whole life was one dedicated to the notion of equity in the lives of the people she had known since childhood—immigrants, refugees and the sons and daughters of those who worked so many hours they never had time to learn English.

In Boston, at that time, desperate patients who didn't speak English would often bring their own family members to interpret. This was not a good practice because family members, whether they speak English or another language, may not have medical vocabulary and may filter out key information in their effort to protect a loved one. The emotional burden on a family member who's made a communications mistake can be devastating, when the interpretation misleads or doesn't suffice, similar to what I later learned when Charlie became ill with a disease that couldn't be identified.

The job at *Sampan* was important to me because of the intimate connections revealed: the intersection of family, place, history, all within a small radius embedded in a large city. My father, the seasoned reporter of immigrant communities in Detroit, read the *Sampan* I sent home every two weeks. When we talked about the paper, my father encouraged me to make sure the articles revealed, through on-the-street interviews and community events, the lives of men, women and children going about their daily lives in a particular place, a particular time. "You've got to get beneath the surface, question assumptions," he said. We can depict a version of a story or tell it from a certain angle, but it needs to be a faithful one, with as many details as possible. Years later I realized he was also telling me that as outsiders, we can't understand all the dimensions of a community. There will always be something we don't completely understand, that we miss. He also could have been proposing, with his characteristic understatement, a way to understand my brother Charlie.

Loss, Again

My beloved husband Neil Anderson died in 2010 from complications related to Crohn's disease, only four years after our wedding and five years to the day after the loss of my father. After Neil's funeral, my dear friends Ruth and Beth went with me to pick up Charlie from his group home in South Kansas City. He was delighted to see them again, remembering both from our wedding. At home, the four of us stomped through our kitchen and all sat down in the dining room. Charlie was beaming, delighted. I wasn't sure how he would respond next. I hated to interrupt his joy. I was glad Ruth and Beth were there. I took a deep breath. Charlie watched my mouth as I stated, very slowly, how sorry we were, but Neil couldn't be here with us today. Neil had died. For a minute Charlie said nothing. Then he repeated what I said, "Neil died. Neil died." He looked at me and asked, "Charlie OK?" This was the most natural question in the world to ask on the death of someone we love, yet I was stunned. How did he know to ask it? Ruth, Beth and I told him, "Charlie's OK." And he repeated it, "Charlie OK."

FINAL LOSS

Within five years after the death of Neil, Charlie was not OK. His life seemed to change when he was abruptly taken off Mellaril and he became a completely different person. I noticed that his body muscles were often tensing up and he had facial twitches along with a mysterious lower pitch of voice. His behavior was just as my mother had once described from the times in young adulthood when he was taken off medication too quickly. The reason Mellaril was discontinued, I learned from the doctor, was that he was showing signs of tardive dyskinesia. What signs? I wondered. I had, along with the group home staff, always looked for telltale indications of the syndrome—spinning, or unusual mouth movements. Had we missed signs that only a medical doctor could detect? We only noticed a change of behavior once the medication had been stopped, not before. In that same period of time, around November of 2015, I learned that Charlie would need to have several bad teeth removed. Possibly, within months to a year, all of his teeth would need to be extracted. Again, we were dismayed for Charlie. How did his dentist miss warning signs of such extensive dental decay?

Something was happening to Charlie internally, but he couldn't tell us how he felt or pinpoint his discomfort. My brother who used to stand behind me as I chatted with the staff and announce, just in case I hadn't noticed, "Charlie's a good boy!" was now nervous and tense. My brother who answered "Forty-nine!" each time we asked him how old he was, even ten years later, was now slow to reply, as if he were tired of the question. He still smiled broadly when I came to see him, yet his robust appetite was gone and he was losing weight.

The group home caretakers and I took him to numerous doctor's appointments where we were told that all of his blood tests appeared normal, and his loss of weight was not unexpected after stopping Mellaril. I found an orthodontist who removed his teeth with care and prescribed a regimen of oral hygiene and treatment that seemed to help over the course of a few months. This extensive dental work we thought was also causing him to lose weight. What we—myself, as Charlie's guardian and sister, and Donna Lunn, who was in charge of the group home and had known him for over thirty years—couldn't do was get Charlie to describe how he felt. We would ask him, over and over, but he would only repeat our questions. In retrospect, I would say that once again we depended too much on words as the medium through which to understand and perceive. Charlie didn't think or feel in words. I made the same mistake, perhaps, as many bilingual speakers do in the moment when their sick family member needs to be understood. They step too quickly into the role of interpreter, with all their biases, love, and firm intentions. They presume how their loved one is feeling, and advocate accordingly. I should have known not to do that. I just didn't know what to do.

I also believed that my brother's primary care physician was unhelpful. He made the point repeatedly that he didn't know what to do because Charlie, as he told us, "didn't speak." True, that was the problem, as it would be for a baby or someone who lost their speech due to a stroke or dementia. The support staff and I believed the doctor could have tried harder, and we kept returning, asking for more tests and guidance. We were not always treated respectfully. Once when I asked how we could track Charlie's weight loss, the doctor retrieved his weight record from previous visits and literally flung the paper at me. I should have complained and demanded another doctor.

The last week of June, I took Charlie to a psychiatric evaluation to see if another medication, a substitute for Mellaril, could be prescribed to ease his nervous tension. That day, I remember, he chose to wear cowboy boots. Later, after his appointment, we had lunch at my house and went for a short walk in the rose garden of Loose Park, near my home. He was walking slowly and I assumed the cowboy boots were cramping his feet. It was the last time I saw him alive.

Over the Fourth of July weekend in 2016 Charlie died of undiagnosed gastric ulcers. He died in his bed, about an hour or so after retiring, at the group home. We'd made an appointment with a gastroenterologist for the next week, but Charlie didn't live to see it. There was never any question in my mind that the group home, with its diligent logs and twenty-four-hour care was more than competent. The support staff were as heartbroken as I was. The Saturday night he died, the staff told me, Charlie had enjoyed lasagna with his roommates, finishing it, along with his salad, completely. His group home roommates remembered him staying up with them a little later than usual to watch television. He laughed, they said, enjoying their teasing banter until it was time to shut the lights off and say good night.

Charles Anderson Was My Friend

At the door of God's House of Praise, we heard crickets chirping in the grass, a perpetual beat in the last humid days of summer. Both Pastor Pardy and her husband were a little cautious on seeing two people—me and my friend Robert—park a car they'd never seen before in the small lot in front of the even smaller two-roomed brick church abutting a Pride Cleaners factory. When introducing ourselves, I thanked them both for letting us use their fellowship room for a memorial gathering of Charlie's friends and roommates. I mentioned the name of a group home staff person who had recommended their center, and they both relaxed.

Pastor Pardy and her husband led us through the church area with its blue pews and decorated altar and into the fellowship center in the next room. Soon followed Juan Williams, the assistant pastor in his thirties who knew Charlie well. He showed us a group of tables, decorated with artificial flowers in small vases. In the front room where church services took place, he made sure we saw the chair where Charlie always sat—first seat in the third row as he joined everyone on Sunday, clapping and singing with the congregation. Juan recalled how Charlie loved that first seat and if he found someone else sitting there when he came in, he just stood by them, waiting for them to move. And they all did, no one complaining. It was clear that this was a place where he belonged.

As everyone arrived, we greeted each one with a hearty handshake. A man who had known Charlie for decades made the first entrance through the door, all smiles, using a wheelchair and helped by one the group home's longstanding support staff. We cheered and applauded everyone's entrance. Everyone knew me as Charlie's sister and Robert as Charlie's friend. As each person entered, we handed over caramel, cheese and plain popcorn and diet Pepsi. The small room became louder and louder, filled with nineteen of us.

Carinne, who had known Charlie since childhood, came in with Lorenzo and their son Elijah, along with Donna, who entered like a movie star. Also, Crystal was there. I regret I hadn't met her before, but I learned that she knew Charlie because she worked some of the night shifts. We showed everyone the collage of Charlie's photos Robert and I had arranged to give them. Josie, one of Donna's daughters who had known Charlie since she was a little girl, had reminded us to sing his favorite song, "Happy Birthday," and we did, loud and strong.

Lorenzo, who drove the guys to Friday night dances, described Charlie on the dance floor—"he didn't need a girl" and how he would start dancing before the music started, even dancing in the van. I told the story of a time Charlie had cracked up when he saw two people in a backyard jacuzzi one December. He couldn't stop laughing, shouting over and over, "Take a bath outside!" It occurred to me, as it had so many times over the weeks since his death, that I would never hear my brother laugh again. Or sing. Or speak in his resonant, questioning echoes.

Later in the day, Isaac, who had ridden in the same van with Charlie for years on their way to the sheltered workshop, entered the fellowship room and sat in the back. We greeted him with a big handshake and a bowl of popcorn. The month before, Isaac had attended Charlie's graveside burial with dozens of my brother's coworkers, roommates and caretakers. There were so many people, the director of Forest Hill Cemetery had to come out and direct traffic. When everyone was gathered, we stood under a stand of trees near Charlie's burial site and shared stories we remembered of Charlie, similar to what we were doing today. It was Isaac who first walked up to my brother's pine casket, laid his hand on it for some time, saying, "Charles Anderson was my friend." After Isaac stepped back, one person after the other approached the casket to touch it, lay a hand on it and echo that same declaration, "Charles Anderson was my friend."

My Brother, the Shape of a Tree

Charlie's oval head fills half the square of a photograph of him on Thanksgiving Day.

How do I fold this image of my brother into how I knew him?

For half a century, my brother's head was the focus of my family's attention. May we be forgiven this long mistake, the belief that a person's existence resides only there, in the brain's wild fissures, unknown as any continent.

In this photograph, light touches the gray bark of two oaks in the window behind him.

I remember one of his first words was "tree," shaped by lifting both palms together as he uttered his version of the word. Charlie spoke his own language, beginning with his body.

Now he has come to the table, where he waits for us to join him.

The photograph marks a Thanksgiving dinner, about ten years ago. On that day, Charlie was patient as everyone kept moving around him, getting dinner ready. We gave him a stack of plates to carry to the table. He was thrilled, a wide smile shimmering across his face. His movements spoke his full presence: his quiet laughter, his fingers stretched out to grasp the plates. He began the ritual only he could perform: first placing the napkin, the fork, and the knife and then laying a plate down gently as he announced the name of each person who would sit with him.

The solemn pace of his movements defined the contours of his soul, as if time had stopped in this pure moment of concentration. An honor to be named by Charlie.

That was one of my brother's many gifts: to sound a name beyond its utterance, to echo an echo.

Belonging and Exceptional Care: A Coda

My brother died too soon, and from an illness that could have been prevented. As much as I knew about the need for language access in health care, when it came to Charlie, I didn't understand the full picture of his illness in time to prevent his death. My brother had desperately needed better medical care, suited for someone with his communication disorders.

What I learned from the experience has compelled me to signal this caution to other advocates for people with communication disorders: always ask detailed questions related to the individual's care and press for thorough medical testing, the same as one would request for an infant unable to verbalize. An advocate needs to be aware of patients' rights. If those rights have been violated, it is appropriate to press for further investigation. The place to start is the medical practice's equity and inclusion office. Another place to follow up is through the region's Civil Rights Office. A brutal fact I wish I had known before Charlie died: People with intellectual disabilities are at risk of dying earlier in life for a range of reasons connected to their health care and living arrangements.

Today, in the midst of a world pandemic, their risk of dying is even greater. In 2021, *The New England Journal of Medicine* reported that people with intellectual disabilities who contract COVID-19 are second only to older people in their risk of dying from the virus. The study reviewed the health status of over sixty-four million people in 547 healthcare institutions. That means a person with intellectual disabilities is more at risk of dying than a person with heart failure, kidney disease or lung disease. A person with intellectual disabilities or anyone with a communication disorder needs as much support as humanly possible from those of us gifted with the ability to speak we take for granted so easily.

There is some good news to share that may help people with autism and intellectual disabilities. Hoangmai (Mai) Pham, physician and mother to a son on the autistic spectrum, has recently taken pioneering steps to bridge the gap of understanding by the medical community of the needs of adults (especially young adults) on the autistic spectrum. She founded, in collaboration with other health providers who had seen family members struggle, the Institute for Exceptional Care. The institute integrates a range of specific strategies in both medical and mental health treatment tailored to help people with autism and intellectual disabilities.

Also, people with autism who are nonverbal and have never had an opportunity to be trained in communications have a new advocate, Elizabeth Bonker, a Rollins College valedictorian with autism who was chosen by her peers to give the college's commencement speech in May of 2022. Bonker presented her speech through text-to-speech software. She has started a nonprofit organization, Communication 4 All, to help those in school with communication barriers to receive special training, such as how to type on a keyboard, training that led to her own mastery of text-to-speech software.

A deeper understanding of the wide neurodivergent community is growing, thanks to passionate leadership by people who are themselves neurodivergent. A good place I've found to start is by reviewing terms that have emerged recently, such as the glossary published on the website of Spectroomz, an organization connecting people with autism to jobs. Additionally, Easter Seals, a nonprofit organization assisting people with disabilities, has listed a glossary on its website with words noted that are not in common use anymore.

To understand how the dynamics of inclusion intersect with race and social justice, extending to all aspects of society, one outstanding source is the Othering & Belonging Institute at the University of California Berkeley, led by scholar, civil rights activist and spiritual guide john a. powell. The institute brings together artists, researchers and organizers to build a movement of inclusion.

National Public Radio (NPR) is to be commended for its consistent reporting on new breakthroughs for people who are neurodivergent, covering not only the two advocates for people with autism mentioned above, but other news on innovative approaches to including people with differing modes of thinking, feeling, speaking and expression.

BIBLIOGRAPHY

Bachelard, Gaston. *The Poetics of Space: The Classic Look at How We Experience Intimate Spaces*. Boston: Beacon Press, 1994.

Dehaene, Stanislas. *How We Learn: Why Brains Learn Better Than Any Machine . . . for Now*. New York: Viking, 2020.

Donvan, John and Zucker, Caren. *In a Different Key: The Story of Autism*. New York: Broadway Books. 2016.

Dybwad, Rosemary. *Perspectives on a Parent Movement: The Revolt of Parents of Children with Intellectual Limitations*. Brookline: Brookline Books, 1990.

Grandin, Temple and Catherine Johnson, *Animals in Translation: Using the Mysteries of Autism to Decode Animal Behavior*. New York: Scribner, 2005.

Grandin, Temple. *Thinking in Pictures: My Life with Autism*. New York: Vintage, 2006.

Hopkins, Gerard Manley. *The Poems of Gerard Manley Hopkins*. Oxford and New York: Oxford University Press, 1970.

Merleau-Ponty, M. *Phenomenology of Perception*. London and New York: Routledge & Kegan Paul, 1974.

Orr, Gregory. *Poetry as Survival*. Athens & London: The University of Georgia Press, 2002.

powell, john a. *Racing to Justice: Transforming Our Conceptions of Self and Other to Build an Inclusive Society*. Bloomington and Indianapolis: Indiana University Press, 2012.

Pinker, Steven. *The Language Instinct: How the Mind Creates Language*. New York: William Morrow & Company, 1994.

Prizant, PhD, Barry M. *Uniquely Human: A Different Way of Seeing Autism*. New York: Simon and Schuster, 2015.

Rich, Adrienne. *Of Woman Born: Motherhood as Experience and Institution*. New York: Norton, 1976.

Roethke, Theodore. *Collected Poems of Theodore Roethke*. New York: Doubleday, 1963.

Rothstein, Richard. *The Color of Law: A Forgotten History of How Our Government Segregated America*. New York and London: Liveright Publishing Corporation, 2017.

Sexton, Anne. *The Complete Poems*. Boston: Houghton Mifflin, 1981.

Trent, Jr., James W. *Inventing the Feeble Mind: A History of Mental Retardation in the United States*. Berkeley: University of California Press, 1994.

ACKNOWLEDGMENTS

My deep gratitude to the many who supported this book as it was in progress: Ruth Buchman, Robert Cole, Maril Crabtree, Jeanne Henry Hoose, Trish Reeves, Maryfrances Wagner and my dear fellow writers, the Lido Poets. I am indebted to Beth Horning for her keen proofreader's eye and to colleague Ajibola Adepoju-Barbee who asked the right questions at the right time about race and inclusion. My thanks also to JVS for demonstrating an example of a caring community. I am grateful to the Wising Up Press and collective for providing their wise editorial advice along the way. Most deeply, I thank the family of Donna Lunn, her daughters Josie Dillard, Carinne Purnell and Stephanie Carpenter, for extending their love and care for Charlie throughout his adult life. I thank Tricia Dillard for her kind support of Charlie and my family.

Portions of this work have been previously published as essays or poems in other formats: "Man in the Moon," *The Boston Sunday Globe* (1996); "House on the Meadow," *Siblings and Autism* (2011); "House Empty Now," *Months to Years* (2018); and "Portrait of a Boy and Beetle" and "My Brother's Roller Skates," the *I-70 Review* (2021). "The Bread of Childhood" titled as "My Brother Recalls the Bread of Childhood" appeared in *Woman with a Gambling Mania* (2014) and "Two Brothers Washing for Dinner" was published in *The Work of Hands* (2000).

The cover portrait was painted by Catherine Anderson. The author's photograph is by Robert Cole.

Author

Catherine Anderson is the author of four collections of poetry, *Everyone I Love Immortal* (Woodley Memorial Press), *Woman with a Gambling Mania* (Mayapple Press), *The Work of Hands* (Perugia Press) and *In the Mother Tongue* (Alice James Books). She lives in Kansas City where she works with new immigrant and refugee interpreters.

SELECTED BOOKS FROM WISING UP PRESS

FICTION

My Name Is Your Name & Other Stories
Kerry Langan

Germs of Truth
The Philosophical Transactions of Maria van Leeuwenhoek
Heather Tosteson

Not Native: Short Stories of Immigrant Life in an In-Between World
Murali Kamma

Something Like Hope & Other Stories
William Cass

MEMOIR

Journeys with a Thousand Heroes: A Child Oncologist's Story
John Graham-Pole

Keys to the Kingdom: Reflections on Music and the Mind
Kathleen L. Housley

Last Flight Out: Living, Loving & Leaving
Phyllis A. Langton

A Mother Speaks, A Daughter Listens
Felicia Mitchell

POETRY

Source Notes: Seventh Decade
Heather Tosteson

A Hymn that Meanders
Maria Nazos

Epiphanies
Kathleen L. Housley

A Little Book of Living Through the Day
David Breeden

PLAYS

Trucker Rhapsody & Other Plays
Toni Press-Coffman

WISING UP ANTHOLOGIES

ILLNESS *&* GRACE: TERROR *&* TRANSFORMATION

FAMILIES: *The Frontline of Pluralism*

LOVE AFTER 70

DOUBLE LIVES, REINVENTION *&* THOSE WE LEAVE BEHIND

VIEW FROM THE BED: VIEW FROM THE BEDSIDE

SHIFTING BALANCE SHEETS:
Women's Stories of Naturalized Citizenship & Cultural Attachment

COMPLEX ALLEGIANCES:
Constellations of Immigration, Citizenship & Belonging

DARING TO REPAIR: *What Is It, Who Does It & Why?*

CONNECTED: *What Remains As We All Change*

CREATIVITY *&* CONSTRAINT

SIBLINGS: *Our First Macrocosm*

THE KINDNESS OF STRANGERS

SURPRISED BY JOY

CROSSING CLASS: *The Invisible Wall*

RE-CREATING OUR COMMON CHORD

GOODNESS

FLIP SIDES:
Truth, Fair Play & Other Myths We Choose to Live By:
Spot Cleaning Our Dirty Laundry

ADULT CHILDREN:
Being One, Having One & What Goes In-Between

CPSIA information can be obtained
at www.ICGtesting.com
Printed in the USA
JSHW080934070423
40069JS00002B/165